FRACTURED FAIRY TALES

BANTAM BOOKS

NEW YORK TORONTO LONDON
SYDNEY AUCKLAND

FRACTURED FAIRY TALES

Told by
A. J. JACOBS

As Featured on Jay Ward's
The Adventures of
Rocky and Bullwinkle and Friends

FRACTURED FAIRY TALES

A Bantam Book / December 1997

BOOK DESIGN BY ELLEN CIPRIANO

Library of Congress Cataloging-in-Publication Data

Jacobs, A. J., 1968–
    Fractured fairy tales / told by A. J. Jacobs
        p.   cm.
    ISBN 0-553-09980-9
    1. Fairy tales—Adaptations.   2. Humorous stories,
    American.
    I. Title.
    PS3560.A2493F73   1997
    813'.54—dc21   97-10569
                                                           CIP

Published simultaneously in the United States and Canada

PRINTED IN THE UNITED STATES OF AMERICA

BVG   20 19 18 17 16 15 14

CONTENTS

FRACTURED FAIRY TALES

THE WITCH'S BROOM

nce upon a time there was a witch named Grizelka who chalked up a very enviable record when it came to witchery. If you don't believe me, just look at her résumé:

SLEEPING BEAUTY
   Cast highly effective spell on young female, putting her in a state of slumber for several decades.

THE FROG PRINCE
   Turned member of the royal family into an amphibian. Received wide publicity.

HANSEL AND GRETEL
   Successfully enticed two young siblings to a house in the forest using sweet food as bait.

Naturally, when it came time to give out the award for The Best Witch of the Year, Grizelka won. At her acceptance speech to the Academy of Witches, she moved almost everyone to tears.

"I'd like to thank all the little people who made this possible. Like that guy I shrank to fourteen inches tall after he said something about the wart on my nose. And I'd especially like to thank my assistant, also a little person, the gnome named Harry. I'll treasure this gold-plated skull the rest of my unnatural life!"

Well, sir, after that, Grizelka's stock soared high, and as far as she was concerned, every night was like Halloween. One day, a typical day, Harry and Grizelka were busy in her cobweb-filled house, hashing out her schedule.

"Okay," Harry said, glancing at his clipboard. "Tomorrow you're due to fly to London to touch off the Year of the Plague. And then you've got a banquet for the Society for the Humane Treatment of Trolls."

"Cancel that till Monday. Tomorrow I've got to lock this lady Rapunzel in a tower and then run over to the—"

Suddenly, the door to the witch's little house creaked open and there stood the most handsome prince in the world.

"Ah, fair lady," said the prince to Grizelka. "Could I trouble you for a flagon of water?"

Such a request wasn't exactly the wisest thing the prince had ever done. In fact, it was tantamount to committing hari-kari.

"Instead of water, try a sip of this!" said mean old Grizelka, handing him a hissing, steaming cup of newts' knees, bat tripe, and other ingredients that would probably not pass FDA inspection, but would turn the prince into a tree stump. Still, witches too have hearts and, at the very last second before the concoction touched the prince's lips, Grizelka's was struck by Cupid's arrow.

"Don't drink that!" she shouted, and knocked it to the floor. The liquid burned a hole three feet deep.

"My word," said the prince. "It must be carbonated."

With that, he made a courtly bow, and excused himself to go to the well outside to quench his thirst. Grizelka stared wistfully through the window. For the next few days, Grizelka just couldn't concentrate on her witchery.

She sent Snow White a poisoned kumquat instead of a poisoned apple. She turned bats into bunny rabbits. She tried to put people to sleep, but just made them tired and cranky. Finally, she admitted to herself that she was in love—but because she was horribly ugly, even by witchly standards, she knew she could never win the prince. And so she went to the magic mirror—which charged only $100 for fifty minutes—and asked for advice.

"Mirror, mirror on the wall—and don't you dare crack on me—how can I win the prince's love?"

"Why don't you cast a spell on yourself? I'm afraid our time is up. I must go before I crack up myself."

Of course! The mirror was right. If Grizelka changed herself into a beautiful princess, the prince would fall in love with her. For two weeks she worked on the project, stirring a cauldron full of wolfbane, mice wings, and artificial flavors and colors. Finally, it came time for the age-old incantation.

"Over the teeth and through the gums, look out stomach, here it comes!"

She drank it and—P☺☺F!—where the witch once stood, there was an enchanting princess. The next day, the newly beautiful witch went to the royal ball. When she got there, the prince and the king were in the corner, talking.

"Well, my son, how are you enjoying the ball?" asked the king.

"Oh, I'm having a ball, Dad."

"I know that, but how are you enjoying it?"

But before the prince could answer, he spotted the most beautiful maiden he had ever seen.

"You're beautiful, you're lovely, you're engaged . . . to me! Am I rushing things?"

Grizelka shook her head. A whirlwind romance ensued. They went to the opera, to the ballet, to beheadings. But there was one little problem. They were never alone. For wherever they went, along came a broom—the broom that Grizelka used to ride on her nightly forays. It would ride in the carriage with them, sit next to them at shows. There was just no escaping her past. The prince began to get a bit suspicious.

"Now, I have nothing against cleaning instruments in general," he said. "I just want to be alone with you."

Desperate, Grizelka decided to shell out another $100 and go to her old mirror on the wall.

"Ah, well, it is all psychological, my dear. You see, that broom over there has a sort of dust complex. Now that you're a princess, it's lonely. It misses its former owner. And it no doubt still thinks you are a witch."

"Well, what can I do?"

"The answer is simple. Get it a gride."

Now, in medieval English, which is what the mirror was speaking, the word gride meant dustpan.

So the witch immediately purchased a small but attractive dustpan and set it beside the lonesome broom in the broom closet. The rest happened naturally.

In the end, when the prince and the princess got married, they had a double wedding with the happy cleaning instrument couple. So, as you can see, not only was there a bride and a groom, but there was also a gride and a broom.

THE FROG
PRINCE

any years ago there was a year that was a mighty bad year for witches. They were everywhere. Big ones. Little ones. Ugly ones. And uglier ones. It got so bad you couldn't tell which witch was which.

In fact, there were so many of them that there just weren't enough people to go around to cast spells upon. It wasn't an uncommon sight to see witches fighting over who saw a person first and whether he should be turned into a duck, put to sleep for three hundred years, or given a third nostril.

Then one day a little witch was walking through the forest, looking for a victim and—Aha! Suddenly she saw a little frog sitting on a log in the middle of a pond.

"My, my. What have we here?" said the witch.

The frog thought to himself that this witch didn't have the highest IQ in the kingdom, but decided to humor her anyway. "We have a frog," he said. "What have we there?"

"I'm a witch," said the witch. "See my tall black

hat and my ugly nose warts? I'm your stereotypical witch!"

"Uh-huh," said the frog. "What do you want from me?"

"I'm going to cast a spell on you."

"A spell?" The frog chuckled. "Listen, lady, I'm already a frog. What else could you do to me?"

But the witch was desperate. She hadn't cast a spell in three weeks. With a wave of her hand—ZAP!—she changed the frog into a...handsome young prince.

"Hey—what's the big idea," said the prince, formerly a frog.

"I admit it's not the kind of spell we usually cast, but you know, times are hard!" She cackled and sauntered off.

The prince was very depressed. He squatted down on the log he used to sit on as a frog. What did he want to be a prince for? He looked at his princely sword and princely cape and shook his head.

He felt his face—not a bit of slime on it! He tried to catch a fly with his tongue. Too short. He even tried to croak, but instead of "Ribbit" he said, "Rather a lovely day for a jousting tournament, ay?" Ugh.

The only way for him to be happy was to find the witch and have her change him back into a frog. You know the old saying: You can take the frog out of the pond, but you can't take the pond out of the frog.

The prince set off in search of the witch. After several hours of stumbling through the forest, he came upon a huge castle. Wouldn't you know it, but this particular castle was owned by a king, who had a beautiful but unmarried daughter.

At that very moment, the king was asking his daughter why she hadn't taken a husband even though she was of marrying age.

"Why haven't you taken a husband even though you are of marrying age?" said the king.

"They're all frogs or something these days," said the princess.

"This young man who just stumbled into our castle—he doesn't look like a frog." The king pointed at the prince, who had indeed just stumbled into the room.

The princess looked at the prince and batted her eyes and said, "Are you a handsome young prince?"

"No," replied the prince. "I'm a handsome young frog."

"See?" said the princess, throwing her hands up in the air.

"No. The boy is just a little mixed up, that's all," said the king. "What he needs is a couple years with a strict Freudian. Or else a wife. Someone like, let's see, like . . . you."

So, over the objections of the prince and the princess, the prince and the princess were married. And they were very happy. Well, actually, they weren't very happy. We're only halfway to the end, so it can't be a happy ending yet.

Try it again. They were quite unhappy. The prince

still insisted he was a frog. He even insisted on living on a log in the pond, which is not the lifestyle the princess was accustomed to. He insisted on fetching her flies, which was not her idea of fulfilling the marriage vows.

The princess pestered him to live in a more princely—or at least human—manner, until he finally agreed to buy a beautiful cottage with a white picket fence. Then one day he was hopping about the yard when a witch—one of the many in the kingdom—passed by.

"Oh, goody!" she said to herself. "A handsome young prince. Probably the only one left in the kingdom. And he's mine, all mine."

She raised her hands, ready to cast a spell. "I think I'll change him into a . . . a . . ."

"A frog?" the prince suggested helpfully.

"Good idea," said the witch.

ZAP!

That night, at the dinner table, the princess slurped her soup and looked over at her newly green, newly slimy, newly tiny husband.

"You know, honey," she said. "You've insisted you're a frog for so long, you're even beginning to look like one."

"I keep telling you, I am a frog," said the frog.

The next day, the frog was squatting in the front yard, when who should walk by but the witch who had originally turned him into a prince! She was a bit upset.

"Usually, when I prince 'em, they stay princed!" she mumbled to herself.

She figured it was time to renew the spell. So, *ZAP!* she tried to change him back into a handsome young prince. But being a bit rusty with her magic, she changed him into a chicken.

A chicken? The prince/frog/chicken had had enough of this. With his wife, who was by now quite confused herself, he waddled down to the Witches' Union Local 143 to put an end to this nonsense.

There sat a gaggle of witches around a table, complaining about the high price of newts' eyes and bat ears.

The former prince and frog stormed up to the table, looked at the head witch, and said: "I've had enough of these hexes! I deserve a little common decency! Change me back to a . . ."

"A prince!" urged the princess.

"Yes, a prince."

The head witch agreed. She raised her hands, and *ZAP!* She turned him not into a prince, but a primate. She tried again. *ZAP!* A prune! Then a prism. Then a pint of pickles. You see, the frog had been so overly bewitched, he couldn't be turned back into a prince. Finally, she returned him to a frog.

The poor frog was very confused. He turned to his wife and said, "Will you still love me even though I'm a frog?"

"Well . . ." she started scratching her head. Seeing her dilemma, the witch decided to put an end to her worries.

With a quick wiggle of her fingers, the witch

turned the princess into a frog. And with that, they both hopped back into the pond and sat on a mossy rock, where they exclaimed, "If we have to stay frogs for the rest of our lives, we'll just die."

Now I don't have to tell you that they didn't die. But every night, they did croak.

RUMPELSTILTSKIN

nce upon a time there was a miller's daughter named Gladys. Gladys had a pathetic existence. All day long, she would spin straw. And all night long, she'd sit up and think how she would like to be famous. Oh, to be famous, with untold riches and men falling at her feet and her own line of action figures.

One night—P☉☉F!—a strange little man appeared before her.

"Little lady," he said, "I can make you famous overnight!"

"Who are you?"

"I am what is known as a PR man," he squeaked. "You know, public relations. Publicity. Flackery. Glamorize the unglamorous. Turn the pedestrian splendorous. Now let's see. What can you do, baby?"

"Oh. I spin straw."

"Spin straw! I love it. Love it."

"What do you mean, you love it?"

"Don't interrupt. I'm looking for an idea. The spark! Of course . . . you spin straw into gold!"

"But I can't spin straw into—"

"Doesn't matter! Doesn't matter! I'll do the talking. I'll just contact Liz Smith."

And so it happened that overnight, Gladys did become famous. Gossip pages, talk shows, and her own entourage of beefy security men who would beat up fans. Of course, nobody had ever seen the gold. But through the PR man's magic—and since it had appeared in all the papers—the people believed it. Every one of them. Even the king.

He called Gladys to the castle.

"I understand you spin straw into gold," said the king. "Well, I am going to put you in a room full of my very best straw and have you spin me a heap of your very best gold. Twenty-four karats, please. None of that fourteen-karat garbage."

"But—" protested Gladys.

"Of course, if you can't, you will be locked forever in my darkest dungeon. And I'm told the humidity down there is awful."

"Oh," said Gladys.

"Not so fast, my good king," said a voice. Who should it be but the PR man, who had magically popped into the castle. "My client isn't giving gold away, y'know. However, she will spin one room of gold for you on one condition: that if she does, she becomes your wife and, therefore, queen."

The king agreed, and signed on the dotted line. So did Gladys. And then Gladys was left to her task.

"Well, now what?" she whined.

"Have I ever let you down, baby?" the PR man asked. And, true to his word, as the girl's eyes widened with amazement, the little man spun a roomful of pure, unadulterated gold. "And now, my dear, our business ends. You are rich and famous. So until your firstborn comes into the world, I bid you adieu."

Her firstborn? Gladys raised her eyebrows. But the little man pointed to the fine print at the bottom of the contract, conveniently providing her with a nuclear microscope with which she could read it. And sure enough, there it said in black and white that her firstborn child must be given to the PR man. Gladys wondered if the PR man had ever heard of adoption agencies, which would seem like an easier way to get kin—but it was too late. She had already signed it away.

About a year later, a beautiful child was born to the king and queen. And sure enough, the little PR man came for the child, according to the contract. What the little man didn't know is that in reading the fine print, Gladys had found the loophole.

"A loophole as big as a Mack Carriage, buddy!" the queen told the PR man. And then she read it to him: "If the party of the first part (that's me) within three days discovers the name of the party of the second part (that's you), the party of the first part shall keep the party of the third part (that's the little kid)!"

Unfortunately, that was easier said than done. (Not that it was so easy to say, mind you.) She spat out dozens of names—from Alfred to Barnaby to Clyde to Zeke—but none of them was right.

On the third night, Gladys was in despair, having exhausted all the names she knew. Just then there was a knock at the palace door. And who should come in but a man who has no importance to the plot other than to get us out of this hole that we're in. He spoke as if he came from a time long, long ago.

"Like, hey, man," he said to the queen. "You don't know me, but I've got to hip you to some news! Like, the other day, I'm walking through this cool forest, when, man, what do I see but this little cat going, 'Ba doo oh bop, she-ram. I am the Rumpelstiltskin man. The king's got his gold. The queen's got her fame. And their baby will have my Rumpelstiltskin name.' "

The next day, when the little PR man appeared again, the queen was ready.

"Ba doo oh bop, she-ram. You are Rumpelstiltskin man!"

"Ooops," said Rumpelstiltskin. "I really goofed."

And so Gladys and the king lived happily ever after, and Rumpelstiltskin was never seen in the kingdom again. There were several reports concerning a young girl who could make diamonds out of turnips, but of course that was in another kingdom. And you can't believe *everything* you read in the papers.

THE SEVEN
CHICKENS

nce upon a time there was a young prince who ventured into the woods in search of game. During the course of the long day, he got tired and hungry. Next time, he noted to himself, bring trail mix. Finally, as it got dark, he came across a great castle. He knocked.

A king opened the door. "If you're selling magazines, we don't want any. Go away."

"Wait," said the handsome young prince, putting his foot in the door to stop it. "I am a handsome young prince who has lost his way. Could you see your way clear to sparing me the bare essentials for a night—say, a thirty-two-course meal, a dozen servants, and a suite with a roaring fireplace?"

The king figured this was reasonable enough. Especially for a prince. And he led him inside to the dining room, where dinner was being served. But there, the prince was shocked by what he saw. For in the chairs around the table sat seven chickens.

Figuring someone had left the henhouse door open—or had taken the idea of free range a bit too far—the prince began chasing the birds out of the room. "Shoo! Scat!"

"Stop that!" shouted the king. "Leave those girls alone."

The seven chickens again took their appointed places at the table and they, along with the king, proceeded to peck away at the dishes of corn that sat before them.

"What's the matter, boy?" said the king, wiping a yellow kernel from his nose. "You haven't pecked a thing on your plate."

"Suddenly, I'm not hungry."

"Awwk, buk, buk, Awwwwkkkk, cluck," said one of the chickens.

"What's that, Florence?" asked the king.

"Awwwk, buk, buk, buk, Squawwwwwwkkkk, cluck, cluck."

"Ha, ha!" laughed the king. "Very funny. Very funny."

"What just happened?" asked the prince, his eyes widening.

"Florence just told a joke," said the king. "Now, son. I'm glad you came along. I've got a problem."

"I noticed. You're a nut!"

The king went on to tell the prince an incredible tale of a witch who came to the castle and cast an evil spell that turned all of his loving daughters into chickens.

"So that's it," said the prince. "Those seven chickens are your daughters."

"No," said the king. "Six of them are my daughters. The seventh one is the witch herself."

"Here comes the plot," said the prince.

"Right. The spell on my daughters cannot be broken until I can discover which one of the seven chickens is the witch."

Well, now, this is the sort of thing all handsome princes dream of. All he would have to do is discover which of the seven chickens was the witch and the king would surely reward him with the hand of the most beautiful of his daughters.

The next morning he got up with the chickens and set about his task. He watched those seven chickens like a hawk.

"It's no use, boy," said the king. "Chickens have the nasty habit of looking just alike."

"True, but they don't think alike. The one that is the witch thinks like a witch."

With that in mind, the prince disguised himself as a beautiful maiden. He figured if he pretended he was Snow White, no witch in the world could resist.

"I am Snow White!" he shouted slyly, as he ran through the castle. "I hope that there's no witch in the castle disguised as a chicken. And I hope that witch disguised as a chicken won't give me a poisoned apple."

None of the seven chickens paid the slightest bit of attention, but an ogre who happened to be casing the castle did. He wasted no time in grabbing the so-called maiden and making off with her to his cave. But just then a handsome knight chanced to arrive on the scene and rushed to the rescue.

"Never fear, fair beauty," he told the prince. "I shall save you."

With that, he flew at the ogre and the fight was on. The knight won out with a combination uppercut to the right jaw and a rabbit punch to the kidneys.

"Ah, fair maiden," said the victorious knight, grabbing the prince-in-a-dress around the waist. "Your lips . . . your eyes."

The prince responded the best way he knew how: a sharp uppercut to the right jaw and a rabbit punch to the kidneys. "Oooh, I like her," said the knight, rubbing his face.

The prince, whose high heels made him a bit slower than normal, finally made it back to the castle and began trying to slither out of his Snow White suit. But before he could, the chickens gathered around him, curious to see what the commotion was.

"Girls! Not now!" shouted the prince-in-a-dress. "Go away."

He grabbed a broom and started swatting at them, hoping to shoo them away. They all scattered. All, that is, except for one. That one snatched the broom from the prince, hopped on it, and flew around the room.

Now, centuries of inbreeding couldn't weed out all traces of logic from the prince's mind. Witches, he figured, like brooms. Chickens don't. That one is the witch!

The spell was broken. And not only did the witch turn back into a witch, but the six chickens were turned back into the king's beautiful daughters, a little plumper and more corn-fed for the experience.

"My boy!" shouted the king. "As a reward, I'm going to give you any daughter you wish to be your bride."

Unfortunately, however, before the prince could choose, the knight who still thought the prince was a fair maiden galloped in, swept him off his feet, and galloped away.

The prince's mother had told him there'd be days like that. But she had forgotten to warn him about the knights!

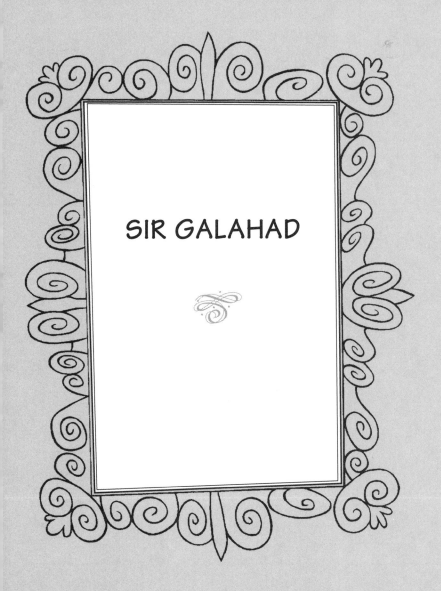

SIR GALAHAD

nce upon a time in the little kingdom of Levittown by the Sea there lived a man named Galahad ... Harry Galahad, to be exact. The world's most famous clown. Big red nose, huge shoes, white suit, the works.

One day, Harry and his wife, Bessie, had a son, and they took the little fellow to be registered with the town clerk.

Perched on a high chair, the town clerk looked down his nose, past a wart, past his horn-rimmed glasses, and asked Harry the big question: "Have you chosen a name for this child?"

"Yes, sir!" replied Harry.

"Sir," said the clerk. "Very well."

And before Harry could stop him, the town clerk had written the baby's name in the town register ... Sir Galahad.

"But that's not his name," cried Harry.

"Sorry," said the bureaucrat. "No changes allowed in the town register."

"But what kind of a name is Sir?" pleaded Harry. "Everybody will laugh at him!" (As if Harry didn't make his living getting laughed at.)

Now Sir—as he was officially known—already had his future decided for him. He was to follow in his father's footsteps, which were about size 34ZZZ, in case you're interested. He was to be a clown.

Sir would come home from school, his history and chemistry books clutched to his chest. "Put that garbage down!" insisted his father. "It's time for us to do your clown work!"

Together they would tromp up the stairs to Sir's room. "How many clowns does it take to fill a Volkswagen at room temperature?" asked Harry.

"Thirty-three and a half," answered Sir.

"Correct," said Harry. "Now if you are given a cream pie, should you a) eat it, b) return it because of the high cholesterol, or c) throw it in somebody's face?"

"It's c, Dad," sighed Sir.

And so on and so on. The problem was, Sir just didn't have his heart in it. What Sir really wanted wasn't to be a clown at all, but a . . . knight. A manly, medieval, armor-clad knight. Each evening Sir would go to bed, close his eyes tight, and try his absolute hardest to dream about being a knight. Unfortunately, it never worked. He always ended up dreaming about something else, like being a member of a singing group called The Pips.

*　　　*　　　*

Sir's mom soon figured out the boy didn't want to be a clown.

"Why don't you want to be a clown?" Bessie asked her son. "What exactly is it that you want to be?"

Out of his pocket, Sir proudly produced his dog-eared copy of his favorite book, *The Knights of the Round Table*, and pointed to the cover.

"That is what I want to be," he said, his chin high.

"You want to be a round table?" asked his mom.

"No, a knight! A knight! I want to be a knight! I want to save damsels! I want to wear armor! Ride white chargers!" Whereupon Sir ran up to his room. His father ran after him, but Sir slammed the door in his dad's red, bulbous nose.

That night something wonderful happened. As usual, Sir tried to dream of being a knight, and this time he made it! *ZAP!* Armor, helmet with a feather on it, the works. He even got a lackey, a short fellow who was to do his bidding.

"Bring me a white charger!" demanded Sir.

Five minutes later, the lackey returned with a skinny, bony pony.

"Uh, excuse me? That's a white charger?"

"Well, Sir William Shoemaker got here earlier and took the last good horse," said the lackey.

So Sir mounted his less-than-perfect steed and trotted off for adventure. He soon learned that riding in shining armor wasn't quite the picnic he had imagined. The ventilation in those suits was nonexistent. Anyway, Sir sought high and low for a damsel in distress. Until suddenly he heard:

"Halp!"

Yes, a damsel in distress. And nothing trivial, either. The damsel had been captured by a fire-breathing dragon who threatened to eat her for dinner.

With impressive valor—and without breaking any rules set by the Geneva Convention—Sir slew the dragon. The maiden gazed lovingly at her conquering hero.

"You've probably guessed that I'm a princess," she said.

"I sorta had a hunch."

And, as you'd expect, when Sir took the princess home, the king was so impressed that he gave Sir his daughter's hand in marriage. The king also gave Sir and his bride a down payment on a small place of their own and before long there was another little knight to feed. And another. And another. And so on into the knights.

There were no more wars to fight and Sir's wife frowned on his rescuing any more damsels. So Sir's days were taken up with his new duties as lord of the manor.

"When you've finished the dishes, remember the moat needs cleaning."

"I should have married the dragon," sighed Sir.

With that, he awoke from his dream in a start. The next morning, Sir's parents were still deeply troubled. Maybe, they thought, if it's so important to him to be a knight, he should be one.

But down the stairs came Sir.

"Be a clown! Be a clown! Dee dee dum dee dum."

And guess how Sir was dressed: big red nose, huge shoes, white suit, the works.

"Sir," said his father, "yesterday you wanted to be a knight. And today, you're a clown!"

"Well," said Sir, "it's like you always say. That's show biz!"

THE TALE OF
A KING

n days of yore, there was a gathering of yokels who lived yonder. In other words, once upon a time, there were some people who lived far away. They lived in a kingdom called Nothingham—mostly because nothing happened there. Street sweepers—did nothing. Postal workers—did nothing. (No surprise there.) Even the king did nothing.

"What are you doing, dear?" the queen would ask.

"Nothing," the king would say. "And you?"

"Nothing. Guess what's for dinner, honey?"

"Nothing."

Yes, it was nothing again, with nothing on the side, and heaping bowls of frozen nothing for dessert. One day, it so happened that a storyteller who had been traveling about from kingdom to kingdom collecting stories came to see the king of Nothingham.

"Here's a story about this guy Rumpelstiltskin," said the storyteller, lifting a sheaf of papers from his bag. "And here's one about some girl called Cinderella. When I get a bunch more, I'm going to write a book and call them fairy tales, then sell them for about fifteen thousand shekels to a major New York publisher."

The storyteller said he'd like to include a story from Nothingham in the book. Now, the king knew that nothing ever happened in Nothingham, but he dared not tell that to the storyteller. He wanted more than anything to make it into the book, and possibly get a piece of the action when it was turned into a movie. So he struck upon a clever plan.

"You wait here," he told the storyteller. Off ran the king to the royal tailor. Ten minutes later, the king was in tights and a skirt and looked like a perfect fairy godmother, except for his heavy five o'clock shadow. Then off dashed the king out into the kingdom. He soon found what he was looking for: a poor but handsome young lad who was working as a hole digger in the fields. (Of course, he wasn't working at the time.)

"Young lad, I'm your fairy godmother."

"Honest?" said the boy.

"Not really," said the king. "I cheat at cards from time to time. But I'm still your fairy godmother."

With that, he told the boy to go to the castle, where he would find the beautiful princess, and that she would become his bride. The lad ran off, happy as a lark, but the wily king took a shortcut and, changing into his royal robes, was at the castle to meet him when he arrived.

"I am a lowly hole digger who has come to marry your daughter, the princess!" declared the hole digger.

"What makes you think the likes of you can marry my daughter?"

"My fairy godmother told me so."

"You get that?" the king said, poking the story-teller.

"I got it! I got it!" the storyteller said, scribbling madly, knowing he was witnessing a scoop. He could fairly taste that congratulatory lunch at the Four Seasons with his agent.

"If your fairy godmother told you, it must be so. But first you must prove that you are brave. You must rescue her from the terrible troll."

"But the terrible troll doesn't have her."

"He will," said the king. "Just wait here."

And dashing to the phone, the king called a terrible troll.

"Hello, terrible troll? . . . It's me, the king. . . . Fine, and you? . . . And the little trolls? . . . Good. Listen, I have a little business proposition I want to make to you."

And after making the deal with the troll, the king hurried back to his throne. "Now, as I was saying, you must prove your bravery by rescuing my daughter from the troll."

And at that moment, the terrible troll leaped into the room, making a horrible sound. "Arrrrrrrrhhhh."

"Right on cue!" said the king, satisfied he was getting his money's worth.

Snatching the frightened princess, the troll carried her out of the castle and off into the hills. "You getting this?" the king asked the storyteller.

"Sure am," he replied. "How do you spell 'Arrrrrhhhh'?"

The lad ran off after the troll, smote him with a stick, stole back the beautiful princess, and returned her to the palace.

"I defeated the troll and brought you your daughter, sire," said the boy.

"Now, there's just one more thing you need to do before marrying my daughter. You must go out into the world and make your fortune."

Once again, the king rushed off and got into his fairy godmother suit. This time, he grabbed a chest of gold from the palace cellar and buried it under a tree in the forest.

"Ting-a-ling!" called the king, signaling the lad. "There's a chest of gold under the biggest tree in the forest!"

The lad shuffled off to find the treasure and the king hurried back to his throne to await the boy's return.

"And then," the out-of-breath king said to the storyteller, "he found a chest of gold under a tree. Should be here any minute."

They waited. And waited. And waited. Finally, after six weeks, a runner came to the castle to bring the news. The runner reached into his fanny pack and got out the message.

"Hey, King," he said. "You know that young lad with the chest of gold you're waiting for. Well, he's not coming. He met a milkmaid from Altadena on the way to the castle and ran off with her."

"Sorry, King," said the storyteller. "I can't write

a story without a happy ending. Too bad. You had a good one going for you there."

With that, the king flew into such a rage that he hurled his throne out of the window and—*WHAM!*—wouldn't you know it, it landed on an evil witch.

POOF! She cast a spell on the king and changed him into a homely little duck. Upon seeing this, the storyteller got an idea and wrote a fine little fairy tale that almost everybody has read: "The Ugly Duck King."

HANSEL AND GRETEL

nce upon a time deep in a large forest there lived a woodchopper, his wife, and their two children, Hansel and Gretel. It was a beautiful forest, full of trees, flowers, and butterflies and streams. Matter of fact, the family had everything they could ever want—except for one little thing.

"Food! I must have food!" screamed the woodchopper's wife, running in circles and tugging at her hair.

But the woodchopper just wagged his finger. "Remember, food isn't everything, dear," he reminded her.

"No, but it's something."

"Listen," said the woodchopper. "We have the trees, the flowers, the butterflies, the streams... what more could a body want?"

"Ummm, ever hear of carbohydrates, amino acids, riboflavin?"

That one threw the woodchopper for a loop. After a bit more argument, he agreed to go out into the forest and try to hunt down some of these carbohydrates and amino acids. (Yes, his wife assured him, they are in season.) But every time the woodcutter went searching for food, a curious thing happened. He just couldn't pass a tree without chopping it down. He'd come home loaded with logs, but no food.

By now, the wife had become so frustrated with her husband, she wasn't exactly playing gin rummy with a full deck. Just listen: "Hey, kids!" she shouted. "Anyone for a roast leg of log? Umm . . . yummy." Young Hansel and Gretel realized it was time for them to take this problem on themselves.

"We've got to go out and get food," whispered Gretel. "Mom's gone a little kookie."

"Kookie!" shouted their mother, overhearing them. "What a good idea. I would love to have a kookie! Mmm. Chocolate chip kookie."

So, taking a few precious grains of parched corn, the children set out for the forest. Hours later, Gretel began to worry.

"Hey, Hansel," she said. "Once we've found the food, how do we find our way back?"

"Easy, Gretel. Remember those grains of parched corn? I've been leaving them as a trail so we can find our way home. Some neat plan, huh?"

Gretel shook her head and slapped her hand to her forehead. "That plan is for the birds."

Yes, you guessed it. Gretel was right. It literally was for the birds. As the kids walked along, dozens of crows swooped down behind them and ate up all the corn. Hopelessly lost, the children wandered about, passing tree after tree after tree until Hansel suddenly bumped into something. Something that wasn't a tree!

"Watch your step, stupid!" shouted Gretel. "You bumped right into that gingerbread house!"

One, two, three. It hit them.

"Gingerbread house!" they screamed in unison. Indeed it was. A three-bedroom, four-bath Victorian gingerbread house in a traditional rural setting. Oh, and the entire house was made of spicy cookies and adorned with candies in primary colors.

"Mmmhh," said Gretel, snapping off a piece of the house. "Have a little shutter."

"I'm more of a shingle and door man myself!" said Hansel, diving in on his own. And in a few minutes the brother-and-sister team had eaten a big hole in the little house. And then suddenly, who should appear out of thin air but a little hunched-over woman with a wart on her nose, holding a broom and wearing a big, black, pointy hat.

"Oh boy," said Hansel. "There's always a catch. You're a wicked witch, aren't you?"

"Well, yes . . ."

"And you've got all kinds of magic powers . . . true?" demanded Hansel.

"Well, no."

"You mean you can't breathe fire and smoke?"

"No. I try but I just get nauseous."

"And you can't summon up demons?"

"I don't know," said the witch, scratching her head. "Let me try. Hey you demons! Come to mama!!"

And just like that, right on cue, appeared . . . a bluebird.

"Some demon," laughed Hansel. "You've got no magic powers at all!"

"Well," said the witch. "There is one thing I'm

pretty good at. And that is turning children into aardvarks!" With that, she pointed her crooked finger at Hansel, and ZING! the little boy shrank down into an aardvark.

"Got to admit," Gretel said. "At that, you're pretty good."

"Problem is," said the witch, "I really don't care much for aardvarks."

"Then what gives?" demanded Hansel.

"Well, I care even less for children. And I've got the witches' tradition to uphold, you know?"

"Isn't there something you'd rather do?" asked Gretel.

"Oh sure," said the witch. "I'd like to know how to ride a broomstick. Vrooooom! But what's the use? I can never seem to get it off the ground."

"If I show you how to ride a broomstick, will you change Hansel back again?" Gretel asked.

"Yes. But, you aren't even a witch. How would you know?"

"Oh, come on. There's a little witch in all us girls."

And with that Gretel snapped into action. "Now you take this broom, and you twirl it all around. Now you put it on the ground. And you sit right down. Now you tell that broom, Va, va, voom! Fly around the room!"

And sure enough, Gretel began to fly. And the witch turned green with envy. (Well, actually, she was already pretty green to begin with, but you get the idea.) She snatched the broom away and off she flew. Unfortunately, the witch had forgotten to ask Gretel how to turn off the broom, so once she started it, she had to keep going. And in a little while, the witch had zoomed so far that she was in orbit around the Earth, where she remains to this day.

But the witch did keep her word, for as soon as she was gone, Hansel turned back into himself. The brother-and-sister team packed up and started off into the deep and confusing forest. Now since they were in a magic forest, they soon came upon a huge talking duck.

"Oh, duck, tell us the way back to our cottage!"

"Je ne comprends pas," replied the duck. Yes, unfortunately, this was a French talking duck. But with his duckbill he motioned the two onto his back. Off they trotted, and after a long time, the duck said, "Voilà! Nous sommes ici!" (That's French for "end of the line.")

Off hopped the kids, and there was their little old cottage and their little old pond and there sitting on a log was their father. But instead of his usual ax, he was holding a musket.

"Father, why aren't you chopping down trees?" asked Gretel.

"Gretel," replied her father, "I've finally realized that all that glitters is not trees! Besides, I've chopped them all down. Now it's hunting! Hunting's the only thing."

So from that day on, Hansel and Gretel had plenty of food, and their mother never went hungry again. Although she did find the stray bullets whizzing around the living room a bit disconcerting.

"Sometimes," she told Hansel, "I wish he'd stuck to woodcutting."

PINOCCHIO

nce upon a time in a faraway city lived a kindly old wood-carver named Geppetto. All day long, he sat in his tiny workshop and carved puppets out of wood with his crude jackknife.

"Boy, this whittling sure gets to be a drag," said Geppetto one day. "Looka me. Talking to a pine-top dummy. If only you was a real kid! I could get you a paper route and take it easy for a while."

No sooner had kindly old Geppetto shuffled off to bed than a good fairy mysteriously appeared. The fairy figured that kindly old Geppetto deserved better, and decided to grant him his wish. She tapped the puppet on the head and—POOF!—it sprang to life.

"Ugh," groaned the puppet. "Do I need a cup of joe. Hey, who are you?"

"I'm the good fairy who just brought you to life," said the fairy.

"Yeah, but looka me! I'm still wood! I want to be a real boy!"

The fairy told the puppet that yes, one day, he

could be a real boy. But as always, there was a catch. The puppet had to perform a brave deed. With that, the fairy mysteriously disappeared and the puppet ran to wake Geppetto and tell him the good news.

"Hey, kindly old Geppetto," said the puppet, shaking the wood-carver awake.

"Whatever you sellin' I don't want," grunted Geppetto.

"No, it's me, the puppet you carved. The good fairy brought me to life."

Geppetto bolted up, clicked his heels, and shouted, "Yabba-dabba-doo!" (Italian for Hooray!) "Oh, I so happy! A talking puppet with no strings? You're worth a fortune! I'm gonna call you Pinocchio and start my own television show."

"But I don't want to be on television," said the puppet. "I want to do a brave deed and become a real boy."

"You outta your mind, Splinters? Stay wood. Stay wood! You gonna be bigger than Hunch and Juicy."

"That's Punch and Judy," said the puppet. But Geppetto wasn't listening. He was already on the phone with J. Quincy Flogg, the president of the television network, telling him about this hot new act. Flogg loved the concept and, after three dozen focus groups, 22 studies, and 158 meetings, he boldly agreed to give Geppetto a show. It was tentatively titled Pinocchio Doody Show and after some hard bargaining, Geppetto got himself a million dollars and two coffee breaks for each show.

Everybody soon got to work. Pinocchio was sent to a personal trainer to make sure his pine was hard but flexible. He got some high-priced wooden surgery for his nose, which mysteriously grew each time he lied. (Which, in show business, was quite a bit.) And he started shooting a commercial for lemon-scented wood polish—no easy task.

"Take it from the top!" yelled Geppetto, on the commercial's set.

"But kindly old Geppetto," sighed Pinocchio, "I've already done the commercial fifty times."

"Hey, knothead, you know what this is?" asked Geppetto, holding up a piece of paper.

"It's paper."

"Atsa right," said Geppetto. "And you know what it's made of?"

"Wood."

"Atsa right again. Now . . . you wanna wind up as a big brown roll in a butcher shop?"

"No, sir," said Pinocchio.

"Okay. Then let's see that soft smile and the hard sell."

Finally, all was in readiness for the big show. Backstage, Pinocchio sat in his chair, his makeup artist applying a little varnish. The director approached him.

"Don't worry, Pinocchio," he said. "If you forget your lines, you can always look at the cue cards."

Pinocchio shrugged his shoulders. He didn't need any cue cards, he said. He knew his part. Now who should overhear this but J. Quincy Flogg, the president of the network. He was stunned. "A TV star not using idiot cards! Why, that's the bravest thing I've ever heard."

It was quite brave. In fact, it was such a brave

deed that the mere *thought* of it instantly turned Pinocchio from a wood puppet into a real boy. But as soon as that happened, the network canceled the show. Geppetto tried to sell his idea to Disney as a nice family movie, but Disney couldn't care less. Geppetto and Pinocchio found themselves penniless and on the street.

Just then, the good fairy appeared again.

"Oh, I love happy endings," she said. "Finally Pinocchio's a real boy and he can be your son and live with you forever."

"You offa your head?" shouted Geppetto. "I want to be lonely. I don't *like* kids. I'm leaving." Geppetto sulked off to his workshop, where he made hundreds and hundreds of other puppets, hoping that one would come to life again someday, which never happened.

The good fairy comforted the little boy. "Let him go. You see, he isn't your real father at all. *That's* your real father." She pointed at J. Quincy Flogg, the head of the network.

Pinocchio was overjoyed to find his real father at last, and Flogg was happy too. He was so happy he gave his son a starring role in the nighttime soap opera *Faraway Hamlet 90210*, even though he had minimal acting skills.

THE ELVES AND
THE SHOEMAKER

 nce upon a time, there was a painter. He was a good painter and he made a modest living for his wife and himself. All was well, except for one thing. The painter didn't want to be a painter. He wanted to be a shoemaker.

"I'm drudging my way through life!" he whined to his wife one morning. "Every day, from nine to five, it's canvas and landscapes and easels and, oh, it's so dull. I want to do something creative!"

"But I always thought painting was creative," said his wife. "You deal with light and shade and perspective and such."

"You call that creative?" The painter shook his head sadly. "I'll tell you creative. Making shoes. *That's* creative. Something for the feet. Something that lives. Something to last through eternity. Shoes that sing!"

But just then, the clock struck nine. Time for work. The painter shuffled off to the nearest still life and, with a sigh, began dabbing and swirling the canvas. "I wish I were a shoemaker. I wish I were a shoe-maker. I wish I were a shoemaker."

POOF! The third time he said the magic phrase, an elf appeared—the patron elf of shoemakers.

"So you want to be like Herman Cappachino," said the elf.

"Who are you and who is Herman Cappachino?"

"No need to explain who I am," said the elf, pointing out he was already explained in a previous paragraph. "But Herman Cappachino—he was just the greatest little shoemaker to ever live. When Napoleon tromped through Russia, whose shoes was he wearing? When Hannibal crossed the Alps? And when Dorothy, that girl from Iowa or something, clicked her heels? Whose shoes did they have on? Herman Cappachino, that's who."

"Oooh," said the painter. "How can I be a famous shoemaker like Herman Cappachino?"

"It ain't easy," replied the elf. "You gotta suffer. You gotta spend time on the Left Bank of Paris. You gotta study. You gotta wear berets and develop poor hygiene habits."

That night, the painter told his wife of his plans. She shook her head.

"Great shoemakers are not made," she said. "They are born. Why don't you forget it and go back to something sensible like your painting."

"No!" shouted the painter, stamping his feet and clenching his fists. "Anyone can paint. I want to sit in cafés, discuss shoelace exhibitions, make loafers in a garret. And above all, suffer!"

So that night, the painter left for Paris. He entered the famous shoe school, Beau Chaussure, and under the tutelage of the famous, if unwashed, professor, Jean-Claude Louis-Mark-Paul, he learned all there was to know about shoemaking. He took The History of the Heel in Eighteenth-Century Brazil. He read all the books on tongue theory and practice. He wrote an essay called "What Those Plastic Things on the End of Shoelaces Are Really Called." But alas, he never learned how to make a shoe that sang.

"If only I could make a shoe that sings of spring, of love. How can I make a shoe with a soul as well as a sole?"

Just then, as he stood on Paris's main boulevard, pulling the rest of his hair out, he heard the most beautiful music. He followed the lovely sound. And there, on the feet of a goatee-wearing man, was a singing shoe. The shoe sang its song, then said, "Thank you. Thank you very much. You've been a great audience. And it's for you, the audience, that I sing. Your appreciation is what—"

"Now, that is truly a shoe with a soul!" interrupted the painter. "I must have that shoe!" He reached down and started pulling it off.

"What are you doing?" the man demanded.

"I just wanted to know where you bought your shoes."

"I got them in Elvesville!"

Elvesville! Why, that was the painter's hometown. He had been suffering around Europe, when he could be home, making shoes that sing. So the painter returned to Elvesville and found that everyone in town was wearing the same exquisite singing shoes.

"Where did you get those exquisite singing shoes?" he asked a passerby.

"Twenty-three eleven South Budlong. You turn left, go about three . . ."

"You don't have to tell me!" exclaimed the painter. "That's my house!"

And sure enough, when the painter got home, he found the walls of his cottage lined with exquisite shoes, all of them singing merrily away. And who did he find sitting behind the cobbler's bench, but his wife!

"Why didn't you tell me you made exquisite singing shoes?" he asked.

"You never asked me."

And so from that day on, the painter went back to his easel every day from nine to five. Eventually, his paintings started selling like hotcakes and he became a very famous painter indeed. And his paintings hung in all the famous museums in Europe. But he never did become a shoemaker and had to be content with just being a wealthy man.

Which just goes to prove. Not everybody can be Herman Cappachino. Whatever that means.

THOM TUM

any years ago in a humble but dirty cottage deep in the forest, there lived a dirty but humble mudmaker. He labored from sunup to sundown making mud, but was very poor, for then as now, the mud market was rather weak. When his day was done, he left the mud puddle and returned to the cottage, where his wife always met him with a hot meal. Which she always threw directly at his forehead.

"Why must you throw my dinner at me, dearest?" asked the mudmaker.

"Because, good husband, I am unhappy," said his wife.

So saying, she served him his apple pie—which she always aimed directly at his left cheek—and shuffled off to bed.

Now, being a mudmaker is bad enough, but being a mudmaker with an unhappy wife is too much to bear. So early the next morning, the mudmaker awoke to the sound of a rooster crowing. Unfortunately, he mistook the rooster for an alarm clock and tried to turn it off, which resulted in one unhappy rooster. In any case, he awoke and quietly stole from the house and crossed the woods to a tiny house made of cheese where it was said a good fairy lived. He knocked.

In no time at all, the good fairy opened the door. "For crying out loud, what do you want," she shouted. "If you're here to try to sell me Amway, I'll—"

"Um, are you the good fairy?" asked the mud-maker.

"Of course I'm the good fairy! What kind of a stupid question is that?"

"Yes, well, you see, my wife is unhappy."

"Big deal," said the good fairy.

"If we could have a son to keep her company . . ."

"All right, all right. I get the picture. With a tap of my wand, I grant you your wish."

So saying, the good fairy tapped the mudmaker on the head with her wand. Fortunately for him, the good fairy didn't get a proper windup, and he suffered only a mild concussion. The mudmaker staggered home as fast as he could.

"Oh, darling," said his wife when he got there. "You'll never guess what happened! I found a baby boy on the doorstep!"

"Hooray! It worked! Where is he!"

"I put him to thimble."

And indeed, instead of going to bed, the baby boy had crawled into a thimble. For he was about as small as you can get. He couldn't even get into Little League. He had to play in Really Little League. Now that's small.

In any case, strangely enough, the little boy just never seemed to grow. And thirty years later, the mudmaker went back to the good fairy.

"Is there anything we can do to make this boy grow that's within the FDA regulations?" asked the mudmaker.

The good fairy rolled her eyes. "Take this magic chickpea and put it under his bed—or, in his case, under his thimble. Now get out of here."

The mudmaker followed the good fairy's instructions to a "P" and sure enough, within twenty-four hours, his son had shot up to a height that would rival any member of the local basketball team, the Village 1476'ers.

"Why, he's seven feet tall!" exclaimed the mudmaker's wife.

"And his stomach isn't anything to sneeze at either," added the mudmaker.

And so, they called their boy Thom Tum and needless to say, the boy lived up to his name. He ate and ate and ate. He joined the Clean Plate Club. And then he ate his plate and joined the lesser-known Clean Table Club.

Then, when he had eaten all there was in the house, he set off through the woods, gobbling up everything in his path. His concerned father decided he'd better go see the good fairy to see what she could do about this.

He found her standing in a clearing in the woods.

"Good fairy, what happened to your house made of cheese?" he asked.

"Some big fat kid ate it, then ran off down the road yelling 'Food! Food!' "

"Oh. That's what I wanted to ask you about," said the mudmaker.

"Well, if I ever find out who that brat's father is, I'll turn him into a toad!"

"Um ... a toad?" asked the mudmaker, a lump the size of an adult poodle forming in his throat.

"Now, what was it you wanted to ask me?" demanded the fairy.

"Think it'll rain?"

"No," said the fairy.

"Me either. See ya," said the mudmaker, waving good-bye.

Now, it so happened, a few miles away, on this very day, the king was celebrating his birthday and among the many fine presents he received was a beautiful fat duck.

"This better be an enchanted duck," said the king. " 'Cause if it ain't it's a pretty lame gift."

Indeed it was an enchanted duck, although it didn't lay golden eggs. (That's another story.) But it did lay eggs, by the dozens. By the hundreds. By the thousands. This duck would not stop laying eggs, and before long the castle was filled to overflowing with white, flawless eggs. The king, who had high cholesterol to begin with, was very unhappy with the situation, and became so desperate that he sent out a proclamation, offering a thousand palooza to anyone who could rid the castle of eggs.

Hearing this, the old mudmaker realized he had an answer to his problems. He brought the boy to the castle.

"You say your boy Thom Tum will get rid of the eggs?"

"Yes sir, sire," said the mudmaker.

And with that, the mudmaker let his son loose and the boy dove into the palace of eggs and ate like he never ate before. He ate them scrambled and deviled, over easy and over hard, sunny side up and dark side out. But those jaws didn't stop there. The boy also ate the duck. He ate the tables, the chairs, the walls, the floor. And then the situation got really bad.

The king, calling for his fastest horse, sped to the cottage of the mudmaker.

"You have got to take him back," pleaded the king.

"Oh, no. I couldn't do that."

"Humor me. I'm the king."

"Sorry," said the mudmaker.

"Take him back and I'll give you a kingdom of your very own."

The mudmaker didn't need to consult his financial planner about that one. *That* was a deal. The king returned Thom Tum to the old mudmaker and the mudmaking family moved to a far-off land to rule over it. The mudmaker's wife solved their son's eating disorder by giving him mud pies, which as we all know is enough to kill anybody's appetite. And to make certain they would never be troubled again, no food was allowed in the kingdom. The people were always famished and so the tiny country was called Hungary. And they all lived happily, if thinly, ever after.

PRINCESS AND
THE PEA

t seems that once upon a time there was a kingdom without a princess, and this concerned the king and his ministers greatly.

"We are facing a severe heiress deficit," the prime minister told the king, tapping a chart. "We must immediately increase the number of young female royal individuals in the palace vicinity."

"You mean," sighed the king, "we've got to find a princess."

"That's what I said."

This wasn't an impossible task. The king once did have a princess, but she had been lost since childhood. The king and his ministers simply had to figure out how to track her down. But just as they got started thinking, they were interrupted by the court jester, Million Laughs Charlie.

"Thank you, thank you. Good to be here, folks!" said Charlie, shaking his rattle. "You know, the other day, I walked into this bar, and there was this Irishman and this rabbi—"

"Please," said the king, "we're doing some business here." Then, to his ministers, he said, "How about if we offer a million gold crickles to the princess when she shows up."

"A million gold crickles!" interrupted Charlie again. "I'd love to help on this project. Do you remember what she looked like?"

"No," said the king.

"Good! I mean, that's too bad," said Charlie, rubbing his hands.

"She was just a baby when she left," said the king. "But I'll know her by the way she passes this test I have in mind."

But Million Laughs Charlie wasn't listening anymore. He wasn't even there. Charlie had run home, called up his date for the night—a lovely maiden who lived next door—canceled on her, and got straight to work on his scheme.

He recruited his friend Clyde, a rather big man with a rather small brain, to help. And before Clyde knew what had happened, he had on a blond wig, a lot of lipstick, and was on the way to the palace to meet the king.

"I don't want to be no princess!" whined Clyde. "These high heels are killin' me."

"Shush," shushed Charlie, as they arrived at the palace front door. "Hey, King. I'd like to introduce you to your princess!"

"Hmm," said the king. "She's got more of a five o'clock shadow than I remember my princess having. But if she passes the test, then I'll know she's the one."

With that, the king led the make-believe princess

to a tall pile of mattresses. Under the bottom mattress, he explained, there was a small pea. If she was a real princess, she would be so refined, so sensitive, that even a tiny lump like that wouldn't let her sleep.

The make-believe princess climbed to the top of the pile and lay down as Charlie, the king, and his ministers waited at the bottom. In the morning, the king and his court climbed to the top and, sure enough, the make-believe princess was snoring away blissfully.

"Ah-ha!" said the prime minister. "This individual lacks the qualities necessary to be a member of the royal family."

"He means," sighed the king, "this ain't no princess."

Charlie and Clyde found themselves escorted out of the palace, helped along by a swift kick or two on the bottom from the palace guards.

"Now you've done it, you hussy!" shouted Million Laughs Charlie.

But Clyde didn't get off that easily. Over the next few days, Charlie dressed his friend up in a red wig, a brown wig, and a browner wig and sent him off to the palace to pretend to be another girl. Hoping to keep him up, he would feed Clyde coffee and tell him scary tales about monsters and politicians. But each time, Clyde would sleep soundly through the night. And in the morning, he would be forced to leave the palace, rubbing his rear.

After several days of this, the two dejected men went back to Charlie's house to regroup. There, Charlie's neighbor was out in the yard, washing her carriage.

"Hey, honey," Charlie said to her. "My business deal fell through. Got some time on my hands. What say we go out and have a bite to eat."

"Sorry, Charlie," said the maiden. "I'm exhausted. I didn't get a wink last night. I think there was a pea under my mattress."

"Did you try maybe reading anything by John Updike?" asked Charlie. "Wait a sec. Didn't sleep a wink?"

Yes, Charlie had figured it out. This really was a princess. The real thing. The girl that would get the million gold crickles and all the titles of her realm. Before you could say "greedy no-goodnik," Charlie had taken the girl to meet the king.

"Oh, darling," said the king, giving his daughter a hug. "Here's a million gold crickles—minus thirty percent for taxes—plus your choice of any man in the kingdom."

"Wow!" said the princess. "Any man in the kingdom?" She smiled, looking over at her escort—and his friend. "Oh, Clyde. Will you be mine?"

"For keeps!" said Clyde.

That's the story. The king had his daughter, the princess had her gold, and Clyde had the princess and they all lived happily ever after. Ooops. Almost all lived happily ever after. Poor Million Laughs Charlie spent the rest of his days unsuccessfully trying to sell unauthorized fairy tales of the king and his court.

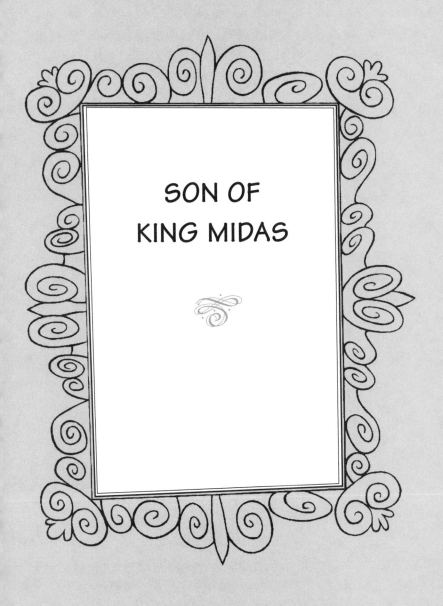

SON OF
KING MIDAS

 ou might remember King Midas. He had a gold mine at the tip of a finger. Everything he touched turned to gold. For instance, that golden statue in the palace garden? Once his daughter. The fountain out in front? Once his butler. Yes, although it was a fabulous talent, it had its drawbacks.

Now, unknown to many people, myself included, King Midas had a son. King Midas hardly knew he had a son, either. On a rare night, the king and his son were eating dinner together. (The king was trying to dig into his flounder and—*DING!*—it became a goldfish.)

"My boy?" asked King Midas. "Why is it we never spend any time together?"

"You think I want to end up like Sis?"

Young Midas wisely decided to leave home. He packed his golden toothbrush in a golden suitcase and left the castle in a yellow cab. (The king hadn't gotten to that one yet.) In the big city, the boy enrolled at a large university and majored in dentistry.

He finally felt free to pursue his passion of studying tooth decay. And to forget his roots—the familial kind—he shunned all things gold. Even his American Express was the regular old green kind. (As a prince, you know, he could have gotten that gold card.)

But fate was about to strike a rather unfair blow. Young Midas was so intent on reading about molars and gums that he failed to notice a change in himself. One day, sitting in class, he asked a fellow student for a pencil. Young Midas took the writing instrument and—*DONG!*—it turned into gold. Not the best gold, mind you. (That would have made a *ding* sound, not a *dong* sound.) But it was gold, nonetheless.

"Darn thing won't write!" young Midas exclaimed to the student. "Where'd you get the gold pencil from?"

"It wasn't gold when I gave it to you."

Young Midas shrugged the incident off. But as you can see, young Midas had inherited his father's golden touch. It began in small ways like the pencil problem, but it really manifested itself on graduation day.

"It is with the utmost pride and honor that I hand you this scroll!" said the dean, handing young Midas his diploma.

And—*DONG!*—the scroll changed to gold— and *DONG!* the Dean went that way, too.

"Dean!" exclaimed Midas. "Dean, what's wrong! You look dizzy, Dean!"

Aware of his dreadful legacy, but still a dentist

at heart, the sorrowful young man opened up an office and went into the business.

One day, young Midas was examining one of his patients.

"Now, remember," he said. "Brush them twice a year and—by the way, who put all those gold teeth in your mouth?"

"What gold teeth?" asked the patient, his eyes widening.

Horror of horrors, young Midas had unknowingly transformed all the man's teeth into gold. In fact, it wasn't long before all his patients were similarly equipped. And business began to dry up.

Finally one day, King Midas tracked down his son at the office.

"It's good to see you, my boy!"

"How can you say that after what you've done?" asked young Midas, pointing to the golden dentist's chair, the golden spittoon, and the golden Water Pik. "I've got a good mind to touch you, dear Dad!"

King Midas spoiled what might have been a golden opportunity by convincing young Midas to visit an old witch who lived on a hill. Young Midas knocked on her door.

"Go away!" shouted the witch. "I have a spell to get out by noon. Very important. Can't lose this account!"

"But Dad said you'd de-golden-touch me!"

"Oh, very well," said the witch. "Go into the waiting room. I'll be right with you."

Young Midas went into the waiting room and picked up a copy of *Jousting Illustrated*, only to—

DONG!—you guessed it. The newly golden magazine was so heavy that it, along with young Midas, plunged through the floor and crashed right onto the witch's head.

"Why, you little . . ." she screamed, running after young Midas, as he beat a hasty retreat.

His next stop was a tiny island, which sat in the center of a great lake. Not one of the Great Lakes, although the lake was eerie. And there, amidst the thick fog, stood the home of an old gnome.

"I want someone to take away my golden touch, and I hear you can perform great feats of legerdemain," said young Midas.

"I don't know about that," said the gnome. "But I can do magic."

It was good enough for young Midas. But as he entered the house, he brushed against the doorjamb and—DONG!—the house turned to gold and the island plunged to the bottom of the lake.

Returning to his dentist's office, the crestfallen lad pondered his fate. And that's when a voice spoke from the chair.

"I should like a gold filling, young man."

"Sir, if I so much as touch one tooth, your entire set will turn to gold."

"Fine by me," said the man, a gray-bearded and big-bellied fellow. "And in return, I shall tell you how to solve your problems."

"How do you know about my problems?"

"I've been reading the story."

And so—DONG!—the man got a mouth full of gold. And then he told the young man how to put his golden touch to good use. No, he didn't tell him to open a muffler shop, although that might have been a good idea. He told him to become a locksmith.

What does the golden touch have to do with being a locksmith, you ask? Well, haven't you ever heard of Goldilocks?

THE GOLDEN
GOOSE

here was once a man who had three sons. The first son was very handsome and very talented for he could play the fiddle with his feet. The old man was very proud of him, for he figured the boy would make a fortune someday. The second son was very strong and very wise and could recite clever poetry while holding huge weights above his head. Here is a sample of some of his verse:

> Out of the blue
> A cockatoo flew
> Boo boo bee doo.

As you can imagine, the old man was very proud of him, for he knew the boy would be famous someday.

But the third son was not a bit like his brothers. He was a dullard and very lazy. When it was sunny, he would stand inside all day humming the national anthem. When it was raining he would stand outside in the yard getting his lederhosen all wet.

"Come in out of the rain, son," his father would say.

"What for?" his son would ask.

"For a while." Then the old man would sigh. "That boy will never amount to a hill of beans."

"Well, who wants to be a hill of beans," said the son. "Unless, of course, it's magic beans like Jack has. I read about that in a fairy tale one time."

Anyway, the old man decided it was time for his sons to go out into the world and make their fortunes, so he gave them each some sour cheese, stale bread, and a cookie and bid them farewell. The first son traveled along the dusty road until he decided to pause by a shady tree for a midday meal. He was about to eat his sour cheese, stale bread, and cookie when a funny little man with a long beard and a crooked nose came up to him.

"I am very hungry, young man," the old man said. "Would you share your meal with me?"

"No," the first son replied. "I need this food to keep up my strength so I can play the fiddle with my feet."

A short time later, the second son paused by the tree to eat his midday meal when the funny little man came up to him.

"Pardon me, young man, but—"

"No!" shouted the second son. "I need this food to keep up my strength so that I can hold heavy weights over my head while reciting clever verse."

"How did you know I was going to ask for food?" asked the old man.

"Because I read the book. Just nineteen ninety-five at your local bookstore. Run, don't walk!"

With that, he ate his food and continued on his way. No sooner was he out of sight than the third son came up to the shade of the old tree.

"Pardon me, young man," said the funny little man. "But I am very hungry—"

"You are? Good! Then you eat this."

"You mean, you'll let me have your sour cheese, stale bread, and cookie?"

"Sure," said the dull boy. "I may be a dull boy, but I'm not crazy enough to eat that garbage, ya know."

The funny little man was delighted, and when he finished the meal, he decided he would repay the dull boy for his kindness. He gave the boy an ax and instructed him to cut down the old tree and then scurried away before the boy could stop him.

"Wait! Couldn't I have a quarter or a magazine or something like that instead?" shouted the boy. But the funny old man was gosh knows where by this time. So the boy did as he was told, and chopped down the tree. And that tree promptly fell on his head, which was all right since the boy was already so dumb it couldn't do much damage. And there, at the stump of the tree, to the amazement of the young man, was a golden goose.

"This is the first time I ever got the bird and liked it," said the dull boy, forgetting that no one was around to hear him. "I'm rich!"

He tied a string around the golden goose's neck and skipped off to the village. On his way, he met a wealthy merchant.

"Welllll . . . I see you have a golden goose there," said the merchant to the boy. "I'd like to buy one of its golden feathers. How about I give you a nickel?"

"A nickel?" asked the boy, his eyes widening. "What, do I look stupid?"

"Well, in a word, yes."

"A golden feather is worth at least six cents."

The merchant agreed and gave him the money. But then a strange thing happened. When the merchant touched the goose's tail to pluck a feather, his hand stuck tight and he could not let go.

"What is going on?" the merchant shouted.

"Well," said the dullard, "this is a fairy tale, you see, and strange things happen all the time."

With that, they continued on their way, the lad in front, the goose behind him, and the merchant stuck behind the goose. They hadn't gone far when they met a robber who waved his sword and decided—although it was against the law and not something you, young reader, should ever do—he decided to rob the golden goose.

But when the robber grabbed the merchant to pull him away from the goose, his hands stuck tight and the young man went on his way. When they reached the village, the sheriff saw the robber who was stuck to the merchant who was stuck to the goose.

"So," said the sheriff to the robber. "I've finally caught up with you, Fingers. You're under arrest."

The sheriff grabbed the robber to haul him off to jail, but of course . . . he also stuck tight. And so it went until an hour later, no less than two hundred and six people were stuck together behind the boy and his goose. As the fourth to last person in line remarked, it was quite a sticky situation. (The others tried to beat him up for that, but couldn't because they were stuck.)

Now it just so happened that the king had a beautiful daughter who never laughed, and the king had offered her hand in marriage to anyone who could make her do so. When the princess looked out of the castle window and saw the long procession stuck behind the goose, she broke out into gales of laughter.

"Haw, haw, haw, haw," said the princess, making a sound that wouldn't have been out of place in a stable. Many felt the princess was more appealing when she wasn't laughing, but the king had to live up to the promise.

"You have made my daughter laugh," he told the dullard. "Therefore, you shall marry her."

"Well, now," said the dullard. "That's a good idea. But won't the honeymoon suite get a bit crowded?"

The king saw what he meant, and called the castle wise man to solve the problem. The wise man—who had a beard, which somehow seems to increase one's IQ—said he could solve the problem.

"I can make them all let go in just seventeen words," he declared. And then he turned to the line of stuck-together men and said, "Everybody who doesn't want to spend the rest of their lives in the dungeon . . . raise their hands!"

With that, everybody immediately let go of each other and raised their hands. And, with that, the dullard married the princess. And lived . . . not so happily ever after. You see, there was a reason the princess had never laughed: she was a natural-born sourpuss, and at least three times a day, she would introduce a rolling pin to her husband's forehead.

"Because of that dratted goose, I'll be hen-pecked for the rest of my life," sighed the dullard, as the rolling pin bonked away on his skull. "And that is for the birds!"

So remember, dear readers, if you ever meet a funny little man with a long beard and a crooked nose, don't give him your sour cheese, stale bread, and cookie. Or else, your goose will be cooked.

THE FLYING
CARPET

very long time ago in a far-off land there lived a very rich and powerful sultan. And each year he became richer and more powerful, for it was the custom of the people—a custom, incidentally, that the sultan came up with—to bring him expensive gifts on his birthday. He had two birthdays every year. That was also the sultan's idea.

One year, on the sultan's second birthday that year, the usual sea of people flocked to the palace bearing gifts—jewels, robes, and furs and the like. (No spices, please—the sultan had an ulcer.) Now it so happened that on that very day, a rug salesman from another land chanced to come by the palace, hoping to sell a rug. The palace guards, assuming he was another subject with a gift, quickly hustled the salesman into the throne room.

At first the sultan rubbed his hands with glee. What a good idea for a gift, he thought. But then he noticed something terribly wrong: the rug had a hole in it the size of a full-grown male baboon.

"By the beard of my mother-in-law!" thundered

the sultan at the young man. "How dare you bring me a rug with a hole in it?"

"It's just a small hole, fella," said the lad. "I mean, this rug is almost firsthand. But if it really bothers you, I can let you have it for half price."

At this, the sultan became even angrier, and his face turned a regal shade of purple. The young man realized he had better do some fast thinking, or he wouldn't have a head to think with at all.

"Oh, what a nice highness you are!" he said. "Ha, ha, ha, ha! You can certainly take a joke. You knew this was much more than a small rug with a large hole in it."

"I did?" asked the sultan. "Oh yes. I did. Of course. Ha, ha, ha. What is it?"

"Get this, big guy," said the salesman. "It's a flying carpet!"

Upon hearing this, the sultan was elated. For though he owned everything imaginable, he had never owned a flying carpet. He grabbed the carpet and decided to try it out as soon as possible. And before the salesman could stop him, the sultan ran to the highest tower in the palace, sat on the rug, and pushed himself over the side. Here is what that sounded like:

"Aaaaaaaaaaaaaaaaaaaaaaeeeeeiiii!" Thud.

The sultan learned that the carpet wasn't exactly as advertised. After limping back to the palace, he ordered the unfortunate lad to be thrown in the dungeon. That afternoon, the sultan's beautiful daughter happened to be picking tulips in the garden and happened to look through the bars of cell 32, the rug salesman's cell.

"My, what a handsome man you are!" she happened to exclaim. "What are you in for?"

"A very short time, honey," said the salesman. "Tomorrow I get beheaded because I didn't bring your dad a flying carpet."

"If I help you escape, you could find a flying carpet and make Daddy happy and we could be married," said the girl. "Am I rushing things?"

"I thought you'd never ask, baby."

The princess hurried to the royal kitchen where she baked a cake with a jackhammer in it, and took it to the lad. He ate the cake—which was rather large—put on ear guards and drilled himself out of the dungeon. He then ran to the city to the first rug shop he saw.

"Quick," he said. "Give me a flying carpet."

"What color?" asked the merchant.

"How 'bout blue?" said the lad.

"We have no blue ones."

"All right, so give me a red one."

"No red ones either. In fact, we don't have any flying carpets at all."

"Why didn't you say so?"

"You didn't ask me. How about a throw rug?"

The lad went to every rug shop in town. He found all sorts of carpets—ones that crawled, bounced, swam, danced the lambada. But not a single one that could fly. In a last desperate effort, he went to a fortune-teller.

"I gaze into my crystal ball," said the fortune-teller to the lad. "I see that you will meet a tall dark stranger . . . with an ax aimed at your head."

"That I know. But where can I find a flying carpet?"

"What color?" asked the fortune-teller.

"Never mind. Just one that flies."

"Well, I just happen to have one right here," said the fortune-teller, reaching down and producing a rug. (It was blue, for those who care.)

The young man climbed on and shouted, "Fly, carpet, fly!" But sadly, nothing happened. "What's going on here!" shouted the young man. "What are you, some sort of terrorist from Hanna-Barbera?"

He wasn't. The fortune-teller explained that the carpet wasn't magic at all. But it could fly—if it was filled with little things that flew, like bees, for instance. If the bees flew, the carpet would fly. With no choice, the lad bought the carpet and a jar of bees and raced back to his cell, where he spent the night sewing the bugs into the lining of the carpet. In the morning he was taken before the sultan.

"Please spare me, Your Highness," he said. "Now I have a carpet that really flies."

So saying, he released the carpet. And indeed, it buzzed around the room, a good five feet above the royal floor. The sultan was so delighted, he immediately freed the lad, who then married the princess, and of course, lived happily ever after.

Meanwhile, the sultan flew on his carpet every day and, even though the bees in the lining stung him time and again, he was happy too. For after all, the carpet was a gift. And everyone knows that "The bee stings in life are free!"

BEAUTY AND
THE BEAST

nce upon a time there was a magnificent golden castle on a silver cloud high up in the sky, which has nothing to do with anything because our story is about an old woodchopper who lived in a shack, but that's a good way to start a fairy tale. The old man was very happy, but he had a daughter who was very unhappy because ...well, she was rather plain. Actually, she was really plain. In fact, she had a face like five miles of bad road.

Anyway, it was time for her to marry, but because she was so fat and ugly, none of the young men of the kingdom ever came to ask for her hand, or any other part of her body, for that matter. Then one day, the old man decided to cheer her up.

"Child, it is your birthday and I've brought you something to keep you from being so lonely."

"A man?" she asked, wide-eyed.

"Nope. A mule."

He pointed to a brown, furry, four-legged, grunting beast. Well, a mule wasn't exactly the kind of companion she had in mind, but at least it was somebody to talk to.

"Hi there, silly beast," said the girl to the mule. "I wonder if you were once a handsome prince changed into a mule by a wicked witch. If so, I could break the spell with a kiss." She smacked the mule right on its lips. It was no use. The mule was a mule and had always been a mule.

The next day the old man instructed his daughter to take a bundle of sticks to the village.

"A bundle of sticks?" she asked him. "What for?"

"How should I know," said the old man. "But somebody is always carrying a bundle of sticks around in fairy tales. You know that."

So the young girl took the bundle of sticks and decided to ride her trusty mule into the village. But something very strange happened. Unknown to her, the moment she climbed onto the mule's back—POOF!—she turned into a beautiful maiden. You know the type: blond hair, blue eyes, a figure like she spends her days doing Jazzercise.

Anyway, when she reached the village, she could hardly believe her eyes, for all the young men, instead of laughing and throwing mud at her, bowed, tipped their hats, and made catcalls. She was still trying to figure it out when a handsome young prince rode up to her on a snow-white horse.

"Ah, fair lady!" he exclaimed. "You are truly the most lovely beauty in the land."

"Why, my young prince," she replied, batting her eyes. "Are you nuts or sumpthin'?"

"With your permission," said the prince, "I should

like to call upon you tonight. How about when the clock strikes the hour of eightish?"

Flushed with excitement, the girl raced home, but when she arrived and stepped off her mule—POOF!—she immediately returned to her fat little ugly self. That night, promptly at eightish o'clock, the prince, sitting astride his white charger, knocked on the door.

The girl opened the door and smiled her crooked-toothed smile—one that made chopped yak liver seem appealing—and chirped, "Hellooooo."

"Um," said the prince, who at that moment was desiring a bit of Pepto-Bismol, or the medieval equivalent. "Is your sister at home?"

"I don't have a sister," the girl said.

"Your aunt then," the prince said.

"I don't have an aunt."

"Your cousin? Your best friend? Your baby-sitter?"

"What are you talking about?" asked the girl. "I live here alone with my father."

The prince, figuring he had found the wrong house, galloped quickly off on his white steed. The poor girl was left standing at the door, broken-hearted and trying to understand what had gone wrong. The following day, her father again asked her to go into the village. This time to pick up a bundle of sticks.

"It'll take your mind off your ugliness," the old man said, patting her kindly on her head.

No sooner had the girl climbed on the mule's back than—POOF!—once again she changed into a beautiful maiden. On the way to the village, she chanced to pass a clear, still pool of water. Looking into it, she saw her reflection and was shocked to see she was now very beautiful. She hopped off her mule for a close look and—POOF!—instantly she changed back into her former ugly self. And then, she suddenly realized what had happened.

"I get it now," she said out loud to no one in particular, as people in fairy tales sometimes do. "This is a magic mule. As long as I sit on this beast, I'm a beauty!"

The girl jumped back onto the mule, and—POOF!—beautiful again. And the beauty and the beast dashed to find the prince. When he saw her coming, he rode up to her on his gallant steed.

"Ah, lovely beauty," he said. "I have found you again. Please say you will be mine so that we may be married."

"Yes, but on one condition," she said. "That I remain on my mule at all times."

Of course, this seemed like a strange request, but the prince agreed.

"So be it, my love," he said. "And so that we start off on the right foot—or on the right hoof—I shall stay on my horse as long as you stay on your mule."

And thus they were married by a priest, who delivered the sermon on a donkey. As the years went by, the young girl was very happy, although the poor mule did get a bit of a backache. And true to his word, the prince also stayed on his horse. And as any good husband would, he took her dancing every Saturday night at the palace, where they were the most striking couple on the dance floor. Or actually, the most striking quadruple on the dance floor.

One day, as the girl rode in the garden—WHOOSH!—the wind blew off her bonnet. Not stopping to think, she hopped off her mule to get the hat and—POOF!—she immediately turned into an ugly, disgusting hag again. Realizing her mistake, she scrambled to get back in the saddle again. But it was too late, for just then the prince rode up.

"Pardon me, old hag," said the prince. "Have you seen my wife? Wait a minute, this is her mule!"

"Yes," blushed the hag, gulping. "And *I* am your wife."

She began to sadly confess the whole story to her husband, but instead of being angry, he did an amazing thing. He clapped his hands and laughed for joy.

This is what he said: "Ha, ha, ha, ha. Yahoo! Yippee!"

"I don't get it," said the girl. "Are you happy to find out that I'm really ugly?"

"No!" said the prince. "I'm happy to know that I can finally get off this blasted horse. You see, I'm only a handsome prince when I stay on him."

And with that, the prince hopped off his horse and—POOF!—he changed into one of the ugliest men ever to walk the earth. He was fat and short and bald and full of warts. His face looked like ten miles of bad road.

"Ugh! You're uglier than me!" said the girl, with glee.

"We were meant for each other!" said the man, as they embraced.

"Just think—no more saddle sores!"

And so, the ugly man and the ugly girl were able to live happily ever after. Which only goes to prove that "A mule and his honey are soon parted."

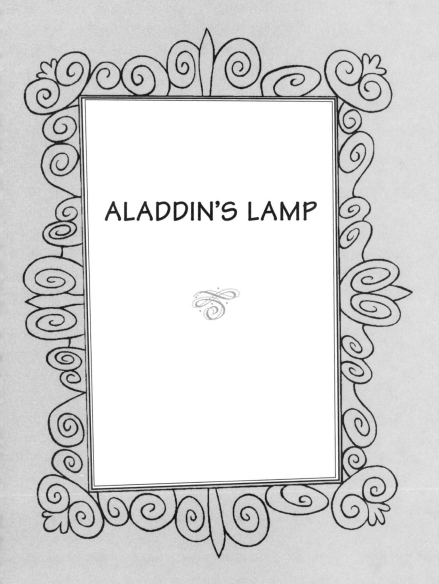

ALADDIN'S LAMP

enturies ago, in ancient Arabia, there was a modest little lamp shop owned and operated by a young man called Aladdin—largely because Aladdin was his name. His lamp business wasn't exactly booming—largely because Aladdin didn't have any lamps.

You see, the place was a front. Aladdin had a pinochle game going in the back room. Then one day, a very rich and powerful king—as if there are any other types—walked into the shop.

"I need a lamp," said the king.

"Sorry, Your Highness. Can't sell you a lamp. How about a deck of cards?"

"Get me a lamp, or I shall have you thrown into a dungeon for insolence. I'll be back at three-thirty sharp to pick it up."

Aladdin considered the options (find a light fixture or spend life in chains) and decided maybe he should get the king a lamp. He dashed out of the shop in search of one, but in his haste, he stepped in a rather large hole and tumbled into inky darkness.

He said to himself, "I seem to be in a bottomless pit." Thud. He hit a hard rock with his rear. "And this bottomless pit seems to have a bottom in it." At that moment, he spotted a dim light coming from a strange-looking, squat lamp lying on the floor. On it were inscribed the words "Rub me and get a surprise."

How could he resist a deal like that? He rubbed and—POOF!—out popped a beautiful girl, decked out in ballooning pants and curly shoes and just a little too much eye makeup.

"Good heavens," exclaimed Aladdin. "A genie!"

"Yes, that's my name. Jeannie."

"That's unnecessarily confusing," said Aladdin. "Are you the kind of genie who, you know, grants three wishes?"

"Oh, heavens no. I'm just an ordinary girl who happens to have been brought up in a lamp. You know, the housing shortage around these parts, and all."

"Are you sure?" asked Aladdin.

"Sure I'm sure I'm sure. Just try making a wish."

Aladdin did. He wished they were out of the pit and—POOF! POOF!—they were. Just like that.

"Can you imagine," said the genie. "All that time I was stuck in that lamp and I could have wished myself out. Oh, the humanity!"

Aladdin hurried the lamp and Jeannie back to the shop.

"Look, Jeannie baby, I've got to check on the game in the back room. You shine that lamp up for the king, will ya?"

"Why not just wish it clean?" asked Jeannie.

"No sir! I've only got two wishes left. I'm saving them for something important."

Aladdin slipped into the back room and Jeannie set to rubbing the lamp that once held her prisoner. But as soon as she began—POOF!—another genie appeared. This one, thankfully, was named Sally.

Meanwhile, back at the palace, the king was in the throne room meeting with the grand wizard, a short little man with a long gray beard and beady little eyes.

"Terrible news, Your Highness," said the wizard. "Your throne has been overthrown. You are no longer king."

"No?" asked the king. "Who is?"

"Me!" shouted the wizard, with an evil laugh.

With that the king disappeared through a trapdoor and the grand wizard sat on the throne and surveyed the plush, carpeted, tastefully appointed throne room.

"You know what this needs?" he said to himself. "A nice lamp. We may be in the Dark Ages, but does everyone have to take that so darn literally?"

With that, the wizard went to the only lamp shop in town—Aladdin's. But by this time, the shop was jam-packed with recent inhabitants of the lamp: Sally, Jeannie, Susie, Jackie, and plenty more. Apparently, the lamp was sort of a pint-sized condominium complex, with all the genies living in different parts of the lamp.

"Who's in charge here?" interrupted the wizard. "I'd like to buy this lamp—although it is a little dirty."

The wizard picked up the lamp and began trying

to rub it clean. But who should appear but—and here's the rub—*the king!*

"B-b-b-but how did you get in the lamp?" stammered the wizard.

"Don't ask me, bub," said the king, who was a bit fed up by this time. "It was your trapdoor. Now prepare to defend yourself."

The king drew a sword. The genies drew breaths.

At that moment, Aladdin, who had just emerged from the backroom pinochle game, saw this impending mess and came up with a brilliant idea. He could stop this chaos—and get out of this pinochle business—if only he wished himself king.

"I wish I were king!" shouted Aladdin. Nothing happened. Everyone turned to him. "Oops," he said. You see, he had used up his wishes back in the game, when he wished for an ace of hearts and an ace of clubs. He needed to rub the lamp and get more wishes!

He lunged for the wizard, who was holding it. The two fell to struggling and tumbling—and both rubbed the lamp at the same time. But instead of another Mary or Jenny appearing, nothing appeared. Instead, something disappeared—*POOF!*—namely, Aladdin and the wizard. And the king was king again. Which only goes to prove that fairy tale endings can sometimes be completely arbitrary.

Oh, and that only in checkers should one try to jump the king.

THE
ABSENTMINDED
KING

nce upon a time there was a king who was so good at his job, he was fit to be a king. Not only was he handsome and brave, but he had paid out the mortgage on his castle. And his carriage wasn't only beautiful, it also got good mileage. He even had a swimming pool shaped like a swimming pool. But for all this, he did have one little fault.

"Oh, honey, dearest!" he shouted.

"Whom are you looking for, sire?" asked one of his many servants.

"My wife, the queen, that's whom!"

"But sire . . . you're not married."

Yes, the king was so absentminded he couldn't seem to remember anything. He had even forgotten to marry. Knowing every king should have a queen, he discussed the matter with his prime minister.

"What shall I do?" he asked the minister.

"First I suggest you put on your pants."

"Then what?"

"Find a wife."

And so it was decided. The king put on his royal

corduroys, and called all the fair maidens to the castle so he could choose the most beautiful to be his bride. They came by the thousands.

"And who are you?" the king asked the 301st girl.

"I'm a beautiful but underpaid servant girl from the country."

"Good!" said the king. "Go out back to the stables and take care of the horses. I think they're due for a waxing."

"But I didn't come here to wax the horses. I came to see if you want to get married."

"What would I want to get married for?"

Alas, the absentminded king had completely forgotten why the young ladies had been sent before him. And though he did hire three maids, a dishwasher, and five cooks, he failed to select a bride. When reminded of this fact, the king was very sad.

"If I'm ever going to get a queen, I'm going to need some help."

So saying, he took a wishbone from his pocket— one that he had been saving for just such an emergency. He snapped it, and surprisingly, got the biggest half, and said his wish.

"Help!" he screamed.

With that, some tiny bells tinkled, a thunderous crash sounded, and an applause sign lit up. There appeared a beautiful blue fairy.

"I am a magic blue fairy and I can help you get a queen."

"I'm all ears," said the king.

"I know," said the magic blue fairy. (The king could have been a body double in *Dumbo*.) "But I can still help you get a queen."

The fairy told the king that his queen lived in a castle on a mountain. But to get to her, the king first had to slay a terrible giant who guarded the castle. A tall order, to be sure—but not quite as hard as it sounded. The fairy gave the king a magic sword that would let him defeat the giant—guaranteed, money back, minus shipping and handling.

The king entered the woods and came face-to-face with the giant. Or actually face-to-knee with the giant. But in any case, the king was right next to the giant, and could have slain him on the spot, but for one thing: he had forgotten the magic sword. The giant picked the king up by the nose and tossed him over his shoulder.

Luckily, however, when the giant threw him, he threw him nearer to the castle. So he actually passed the obstacle.

"Lucky for me. Okay. Now let's go get the princess."

"Not so fast," cautioned the fairy. "Next you must pass through the huge, vicious thornbush that surrounds the castle."

"Vicious thornbush? There must be a catch."

"As a matter of fact, there is. The secret is to be brave. The thorns will part to let a brave man pass."

With that, the king steadied himself, and with all the speed he could muster, he ran headlong toward the vicious thorns. But also, true to form, he forgot to be brave. He chickened out. And that was not good for the king. He got ripped and scratched and poked. All his clothes were torn—except for his pants, of course, which he had forgotten to put on.

"Oh, well," sighed the fairy. "You did it again. But never mind. I'll just wave my magic wand and make those old vicious thorns disappear."

"Hey, why didn't you tell me you could do that before?"

"You didn't ask me."

And the fairy waved the wand and—POOF!—the thornbushes disappeared. Now the king was really ready to go get his queen. But his troubles weren't over yet. This being a fairy tale, he had yet another test. He had to do away with the wicked witch who guarded his love.

"Okay," said the king to the fairy. "What's the gimmick with the wicked witch?"

"I will give you a magic word that will make her disappear."

"And that is . . . ?"

"Fundervogel!"

"Wouldn't you know it. And me with the lousy memory."

So, armed with the magic word, the king ran into the castle and found the wicked witch standing guard over his beautiful queen-to-be. Not expecting visitors, the witch hadn't had time to touch up her warts, so she was very unhappy to see the king. She decided to turn him into a toad, and began to cast a spell.

"Iggilty piggilty, my black hen . . ."

"Wait!" shouted the king. "I have a magic word that will make you disappear. And it is . . . uh . . . And it is . . ."

"Get on with it."

"And it is . . . Fundervogel!"

It was a miracle. The king had remembered the

word and the wicked witch disappeared in a cloud of green smoke. But so happy was the king that he had finally remembered something, he completely forgot about the girl. He ran out of the castle, whistling gleefully and clicking his heels.

Weeks went by, and of course, the absentminded king wandered around the countryside and failed to return to his kingdom, for he was unable to remember which kingdom was his. He finally chanced to pass a lovely young girl from whom he asked directions. And when she put her dainty finger to her chin to think over the question, the king noticed a little string tied around her finger.

"Pardon me," said the king. "I couldn't help noticing that little string tied around your finger. What's it for?"

"Why, to help remember."

"Remember what?"

"I don't know. . . . I forgot."

The girl, you see, was as absentminded as the king, and needless to say that with such a common bond, they fell in love. And so it was that what's-his-name married what's-her-name in a who's-its. And lived in a what-cha-ma-call-it happily ever. . . Oh, forget it.

THE GOBLINS

 long, long, long time ago, a little kingdom sat perched on top of a high mountain. The king of the kingdom was constantly trying to raise money for things he thought the country needed. Like, for instance, another robe for the king.

"That robe—the one with the lion fur around the collar?" the king told his prime minister. "Got to have it. I'll have to levy another tax on the little people."

"But we already have a tax on everything, Your Majesty," said the prime minister. "What can you tax them for?"

"Easy! I'll just tax them for being little people."

And so the king levied a tax on all people under four feet six. Problem was, there weren't that many people that little. Matter of fact, only one family in the kingdom was under four feet six. The Goblins. And they didn't like it a bit.

"We may not have height, but we got heart!" father Goblin told the tax collector who banged on his door. "We may not have altitude, but we got attitude. We may not have—"

"All right, I got the point," said the tax collector. "But if you're going to live on this mountain, you gotta pay the tax."

"Well, then," said the goblin, "we won't live on the mountain. We'll live *in* the mountain."

And with that, the entire Goblin family entered a hole in the side of the mountain and slammed the door shut, vowing to come out only on moonlit nights to try to get the big people. But as we said, that was a long, long, long time ago. After many years passed by, the kingdom entered the era officially known as a long time ago. (We'll skip the era called a long, long time ago.) Anyway, a long time ago, the goblins still lived inside the mountain and still sallied forth to try to get people. Although, it should be said they had never actually gotten a person, and wouldn't really know what to do if they did.

The reason the goblins had never actually gotten someone was that they had a weakness: poetry. Repeat a couple of lines—something like "One, two, buckle my shoe, three, four, shut the door"—and the goblins were stopped cold. Repeat a couple more lines—for instance, "I should have been a pair of ragged claws scuttling across the floors of silent seas"—and the goblins ran away, screaming.

One day, the new king was teaching his daughter, Irene, the facts of life.

"And remember, the goblins will get you if you don't watch out!"

"Oh, yeah?" said Irene. "Have you ever seen a goblin?"

"Umm, no, but . . ."

"Well, how do you know there are even such

things as goblins? Is that a goblin?" asked Irene, pointing to a red couch.

"No, but—"

"Is *that* a goblin?" asked Irene, pointing to a brass candlestick.

"Um, no."

"Is *that* a goblin?" asked Irene, pointing to a little, four-foot, three-inch man with an evil glint in his eyes.

"Why, yes," said the king. "I believe that *is* a goblin."

And with that, the goblin began chasing Princess Irene around the castle and out the door and over the moat and into the kingdom.

"I'm gonna get you!" the goblin cackled.

"I don't want to be got! I don't want to be got!" shouted Irene.

Things looked bad for the princess until she bumped into a young miner named Curdy, and he was so struck by the princess's beauty that he was moved to poetry.

"Oh, Princess fair," said Curdy. "Your golden hair. Upon your head. I see it there."

And of course, that stopped the goblin in his tracks, for he just couldn't stand poetry.

"You saved me with your poem," said the grateful princess to the miner. "Are you a handsome prince in disguise?"

"No, I'm just a miner boy," said the ever-modest Curdy. "Although for a lonely miner, I'm quite courageous and have excellent hygiene."

"Oh," said the crestfallen princess. "Couldn't you go somewhere to learn to be a prince?"

"Like where?" asked Curdy.

"How 'bout Princeton?"

Oooof. That kind of talk makes the poetry seem appealing. Anyway, little did the princess know that the goblin who had chased her was himself a prince, the Prince of Goblins, and that he was determined to make her his bride. And so a pack of goblins—led by Prince Goblin—burrowed underneath the mountain precisely to the spot where the princess was, and popped up.

Actually, they made a slight miscalculation. They popped up in the middle of a croquet court. After a hasty retreat and a couple of aspirin (those croquet mallets aren't made of rubber, you know), the goblins tried again. They popped up and grabbed the princess! Well, actually, there was another slight miscalculation. They grabbed the hygienic miner instead.

"You fellows have made a terrible mistake," protested Curdy, as he was dragged into the mountain. "I'm Curdy!"

"You sure are, hon!" giggled the prince, not knowing what *curdy* meant, but thinking it sounded rather appealing.

So Curdy figured he would just recite a poem and make these goblins disappear. But without the princess to inspire him, Curdy couldn't think of a single rhyme. He could only think of words like *orange*. And *month*.

In no time at all, Curdy found himself in a very embarrassing position. Namely, standing next to Prince Goblin, dressed in a bridal gown.

"Do you take this earthling to be your lawful

wedded wife?" a four-foot, two-inch minister asked the prince.

"Um, could you give me a second on that one?" requested the prince. "She looks a bit different than I remembered her." The prince decided to take Curdy out into the daylight for a closer look. Out they popped and who should Curdy see just outside the hole, but the princess herself. Finally inspired, Curdy burst into verse.

"What a gladsome fine surprise, to see you with mine eyes," he recited.

The prince winced and cupped his ears.

"I love you more, my lovely princess, than pies of apples or minces."

At this, the prince could stand no more. He let go of Curdy and fled back to the mountain forever.

The king was overjoyed to have his daughter back where she belonged.

"See," he said. "I told you the goblins will get you if you don't watch out."

"But you were wrong!" shouted Irene. "It's the love bug that gets you if you don't watch out."

Now *that's* a happy ending.

CUTIE AND
THE BEAST

here once lived an old man who had nothing to do. It wasn't that he was a loafer. He was a clockmaker. The only trouble was that clocks hadn't been invented yet, so none of the clever little clocks that he made worked. And making clocks that don't work is really nothing to do.

He was very lonely. To pass the time, he would play hide-and-seek with himself.

"Three, two, one!" he would shout. "Ready or not, here I come!" And he would search behind the bed, behind the dresser, behind the desk, but he could never find himself. "Where could I be!" he would shout, tearing at his hair. Not a very happy existence.

But one day something changed all that. He was in the woods gathering nuts for winter when he chanced to see a box that was partially hidden behind a large tree.

"A box!" he shouted. "Hooray! I will take it home and turn it into a clock that doesn't work!"

But as he came around the tree, his eyes

widened with surprise. The box had something in it. Something with legs and arms and a head.

"Who are you?" asked the old man.

"I'm a baby who has been left here in the woods by my wicked stepmother," said the something.

"Baby?" asked the old man. "How old are you?"

"Sixteen."

So she wasn't the youngest babe in the woods. But the old man took pity on her anyway, and carried her home to raise as his own daughter. Then one day, exactly a year to the day after he found her in the box, the old man turned to the girl.

"Cutie Lou," he said. (He called her Cutie Lou because she was indeed cute—you know, the medieval version of a supermodel.) "Cutie Lou—this is your birthday, and I'm going to go out and find you a gift."

He set off into the wilderness and soon came to a soft wooded glade. There he found some beautiful flowers made of solid gold—or at least gold plating. Perfect, he figured, for his daughter's hair. But no sooner had he picked one of the flowers when, with a mighty roar, a great beast suddenly jumped from a nearby thicket.

"You are picking my flowers!" growled the beast, who was big and hairy and ugly, not unlike certain senators. "For that I will eat you."

"But," protested the old man, "I only picked one!"

"So, I'll only eat you once."

The old man pleaded for his life. "Listen," said the man. "I'll give you a present. How about a clock that doesn't work?"

"What else you got?" asked the beast.

"Nothing. Only my cute little daughter."

This caused the beast to stop and think, for he was lonely and unhappy as beasts go. He put his arm around the old man and gave him his best beastly smile.

"Listen, terrified old man," said the beast. "Tell you what I'm gonna do. I'm gonna do this 'cause I like you, and I think you like me. I think we really have a bond here, you know?" And then the beast said some things only the old man could hear. We'll have to find out later.

Soon the old man arrived back at the house.

"Do I have a surprise for you!" he told his daughter, Cutie.

"What is it?" she asked, breathless.

"I gave you to a beast!" he said.

With that, the girl started to head for the door, ready to climb back in a box and abandon herself in the woods again. But the old man quickly explained it wasn't as bad as it seemed. The beast, you see, didn't really think he was a beast at all. He thought he was a handsome prince who was bewitched and all he needed was to be kissed by a beauty—or at the very least by a cutie. The beast had read something like that somewhere. (For those of you who are curious, that's what the beast and the man were talking about back in the wooded glade.)

"Hmm," said the cutie. "If he really is a handsome prince, we could get married and live happily forever after. In a castle, yet. And we could send our kids to the best school and I could drive the carriage-pool once a week and . . ."

In any case, the girl agreed and soon found herself in the forest glade, where the beast had been anxiously awaiting.

"Well, let's get it over with," she said. And she kissed him on the left, furry cheek to break the spell.

"Strange," said the beast. "I didn't hear bells or whistles or see fireworks or anything. How do I look?"

"Horrible," said the girl. "Nothing happened. Maybe I kissed the wrong cheek."

So she kissed him on the right, even furrier, cheek. Still nothing.

"Maybe," reasoned the girl, "you've got a different kind of spell. Like amnesia or something. Perhaps a swift blow on the head."

Willing to try anything, the beast agreed and Cutie, with a large, knotty oak branch in hand, got a good windup and—WHAM!—tried to break that spell. This time there was a change. The beast was still a beast—only now he had a beastly headache.

Cutie decided if he was ever going to change back into a prince, he needed some professional help. So she took the beast to the kingdom's wise man. He had an office downtown.

The wise man led the beast through a waiting room and onto a couch. The wise man took up a pen and pad. "Now, how long have you had this feeling that you're a bewitched beast?" he asked.

"It started when I was a little monster only five years old," said the beast. Seven hours—and $800—later, the wise man came into the waiting room, where Cutie was flipping through the latest issue of *Castle and Garden*.

"I wish to announce that he is cured!" said the wise man.

"You mean, he's a handsome prince now?" asked Cutie.

"No . . . but he thinks he is."

And with that, the beast dashed out, wearing a robe, a crown, and a toothy smile. He grabbed Cutie around the waist and gave her his best Fred Astaire–Ginger Rogers dip.

"Alas, fair maiden. It is I . . . Prince Charming!" said the beast.

Cutie rolled her eyes. She had to make one last desperate effort. Knowing that it is witches that cast these spells, she rushed the beast to a local witch.

"I've never turned any princes into beasts, honey," said the witch. "I'm more the poisoned apple type. Did you see the job I did on Snow White?"

"Never mind," said Cutie. "Is there anything you can do?"

"Well, I can give him a shot of my witch's brew. Although it could keep him up at night—it's caffeinated."

The beast didn't mind. He dipped a cup into the giant, boiling pot, and gulped it down in one gulp. The earth began to tremble. There was a flashing of blue lights. And then a huge, roaring explosion.

But there was no change. He was still a beast and always would be. Cutie was very sad—and, so, said the beast, was he.

"I'm very sad," said the beast. "But thanks for all your trouble. See ya!" With that, he bent down on one knee and kissed Cutie's hand. And that's when something completely unexpected happened. In a blinding flash, Cutie turned into a beast. For it was

Cutie who was the bewitched one. She was a girl beast all along. And so, as is usually the case, it was a happy ending. They were married, and as far as anybody knows, are still living a beastly happy existence to this very day.

PRINCE HYACINTH
AND THE DEAR
LITTLE PRINCESS

h, yes. "Prince Hyacinth and the Dear Little Princess." Just about the longest title we've had yet. At any rate, in the kingdom of Normandy, located near Third and LaBrea, there lived a king, named Dum the Seventy-third. You see, that's how kingdoms get their names. From a king named Dum. Funny, huh?

But on to more serious matters. King Dum was miserable, for he was in love with a beautiful queen who had a little problem.

"I'm in love with you, beautiful queen," said King Dum. "But you're a little mixed up, you know what I mean?"

Yes, she was a little mixed up, for she was under an enchantment. And she also had a terrible stuffed nose.

"Honey," whined the queen, "I can't get out from under this enchantment. It just keeps hangin' on."

"Enchantment? Ha! That garbage went out with the Hula Hoop. Next thing you'll be tellin' me you see fairies. Like that one."

For at that moment, a fairy appeared right in front of the king's face, which now contained a rapidly dropping jaw.

"You stop that," scolded the fairy, who for some reason spoke with a thick Brooklyn accent. "If it weren't for our business agent I'd turn you into a frog."

"Your business agent?" asked the king.

"Yeah. International Fairies' Guild, Local Forty-two! But my call sheet says I'm supposed to help you out instead. So what's to help?"

"Well, it's about the queen. She thinks she's under some kind of enchantment."

"She got a cat?" said the fairy.

"Yeah," replied the king.

"Step on its tail."

At that, the fairy took out his walkie-talkie—or in this case, walkie-flyie—and told his leader the mission was completed.

"Roger, Fairy number Fifty-three," squawked a voice over the walkie-talkie. "This is Red Fox Leader. Go to Third and Spring. Woman having a bad hair day. Ask for Rapunzel. Over and out."

King Dum returned to the bedside of the queen, who was busy blowing her nose.

"How are you, dear?" he asked.

"Enchanted," replied the queen, shaking her head. "Nothing helps. Not gargling. Not aspirins. Not VapoRub. Nothing."

"What would happen if I stepped on your cat's tail? Would that help?"

"Are you out of your mind?" asked the queen.

"I didn't think it was a good idea." Crestfallen,

the king turned to go and, of all things, accidentally stepped on the cat's tail. Now, this being a fairy tale, the cat was an enchanted cat, and—P☺☺F!—it turned into a seven-foot-tall man with a turban.

"I am Genie number Seventy-seven," said the genie to King Dum. "Look here. You will marry the queen and have a son with a nose like a casaba melon. And until he says the words 'I got a nose like a casaba melon,' he'll have a nose like a casaba melon. Got that?"

"Seems a little harsh," said King Dum.

"And one more thing," added the genie. "If anybody tells him the magic words ahead of time, they shall perish. Like instantly. Understand?"

And with that, the genie vanished. What's more, the queen was no longer under her enchantment. And so the king and the queen lived happily ever after, until their first son was born. At which time the king turned into a frog and was never heard from again. (That's what happens when a character is no longer important to the plot.)

Anyway, the queen, who is still important to the plot, decided to name the prince not Dum the Seventy-fourth, but Hyacinth the First.

"Isn't he just like a sweet little hyacinth?" the queen asked the adoring crowd at his cribside. "Look at those two cute little eyes and his sweet little mouth and his sweet . . . little . . . button . . . nose."

But it didn't look like a button at all. It looked more like an entire jacket. Or more specifically, it looked like a casaba melon.

"Haw! Haw! Haw!" laughed the crowd, pointing to the baby's oversized nose.

"Silence," shouted the queen. "No one shall make fun of my little Hyacinth." And so the queen declared that from that day forward, everybody in the kingdom would wear a false nose just as big as the prince's. And they did.

All went smoothly until one day the prince decided he wanted to find a girlfriend. It was, after all, his thirty-fifth birthday. The next day, at the request of the queen, every girl in the kingdom was lined up outside the castle, all wearing their false noses.

One by one they came in to meet the prince. And one by one, he dismissed them. But then came a dear little princess whose name was, uh, Dear Little Princess.

And in she came to meet the prince—but of all things, she had forgotten to put on her false nose!

"Oh my!" she exclaimed. "I must have left my false nose at the dry cleaner's!"

"I'll have your pretty little head for this!" shouted the queen.

By this time, the prince was completely confused. He didn't understand all this talk about false noses. But he was clear about one thing: he had finally found the girl of his dreams. After all, he figured, there was room in this world for all types—big-nosed and small-nosed alike. He tried to kiss Dear Little Princess, but no matter how he turned his head, his nose got in the way.

"Oh, silly Prince, why don't you take it off?" asked the princess.

"Take off my nose?" said the prince. "Very witty. How exactly would I do that?"

At that point, all the members of the prince's

court—who had been standing around watching the proceedings—shouted in unison, "This is how you take off your nose!" And they simply took off their noses.

The prince's world came crashing down. He realized he had been living in a big-nosed fool's paradise. But who should comfort him but Dear Little Princess.

"But Your Highness," she said, "you know there's room for all kinds of noses. Small. Big."

"Big?" said the prince. "My nose is incredible. I've got a nose like a casaba melon."

P⊗⊗F! Who should appear but Fairy number Fifty-three.

"Sign here please," he instructed the prince, who did. And with a *KAZAM!* the nose shrank down to practically a normal-sized nose. And so the newly handsome prince and the always beautiful princess were married and all lived happily ever after. Except for the fairy, who had another emergency. It seems the frog wasn't an enchanted prince after all.

SON OF
RUMPELSTILTSKIN

nce, a very long time ago, in a forest, there was a tree—which is a nice thing to have in a forest. Now, in this tree there happened to live a funny little man in a green suit with a pointed cap. He lived with his son—also a funny little man in a green suit with a pointed cap.

One day the son walked over to his father's side of the branch with a question he had been wondering about for fifty years. (He hadn't wanted to rush things.)

"How come we've got to live in a tree?" he asked.

"Because we're not ordinary folks, boy," replied the older little man, wagging his wisdom-filled finger. "We're magic."

"Magic?"

"Yup," said the father. "You know how sometimes folks get into trouble and then they meet a funny little man who makes a deal to help 'em out? And he does a little magic and then later on, they write a fairy tale about it?" He pulled a fairy-tale book out of his cap and pointed to some funny little men. "Funny little men. That's us."

And then, being that it was the son's six hundredth birthday, the father told him it was time he go out in the world and make a name for himself.

"If I do real good," asked the son, "will they write a fairy tale about me?"

"Without a doubt," said the father, who then gave his son a helpful kick on the rear to start him on his way. Off went the son to make a name for himself and, with any luck, sell his life story to a fairy-tale agent for a goodly sum.

In the village nearby, there was a miller who was very poor, but as luck would have it, he had a very beautiful daughter. One day the miller's daughter was carrying a load of flour when who should she bump into but the king himself, out for his daily constitutional. The king was knocked on his royal rear, but before he could gather his thoughts and banish the girl from the kingdom forever, the miller bounded to the rescue.

"This daughter of mine can spin gold out of straw," boasted the miller. He pointed to his lovely flaxen-haired girl.

"Spin gold out of straw?" exclaimed the king, his regal red eyebrows arching. "Bring this girl to my castle tomorrow and if she can do as you say, I shall take her for my bride. Good day."

The king marched off to do royal things, such as sit on his throne and behead people, leaving the father and daughter alone.

"Father, what did you tell him a thing like that for?" cried the daughter.

"So that he'll marry you and we can live in a palace in comfort and every whim catered to, including dental care," said the miller.

"But I can't spin gold out of straw—you know that!"

"Yeah, I know it. And you know it. But the king doesn't know it! And we sure won't tell him!" The miller laughed loudly at his own wit, leaving the daughter with no choice but to bonk him on the head with a sack of flour.

The next morning, the king placed the unfortunate miller's daughter in a dark room in the castle with nothing but a spinning wheel and a stack of straw.

"Now spin that straw to gold—or else!" ordered the king. Thereupon, he thoughtfully gave the girl her privacy by gently closing the door and nailing it shut.

Alone in the room, the miller's daughter sat down and put her chin in her hands. "I don't want to be or elsed!"

The funny little man in the green suit with a pointed cap—the one trying to make a name for himself—had heard about the young girl's plight, and knew that this was the chance that he had been waiting for. So into the room he hopped.

"Who are you?" exclaimed the girl.

"I'm a funny little man in a green suit."

"You could say that again."

"I'm a funny little man in a—"

"Never mind," said the daughter, who had no time for such shenanigans. After all, she was busy doing nothing. "What do you want?" she asked.

"I will spin that straw to gold for you if you will give me your first child after you become queen."

"My first child? Why that?"

"Who knows?" The little man shrugged. "Makes the plot better."

Not one to interfere with the plot, the miller's daughter shook hands with the little man. He jumped to the wheel and in no time at all had spun a room full of bright, shimmering gold. When in the morning the king found everything as he had wished, he was overjoyed. He now had so much money he could be king. That is, if he weren't king already.

They were married, and the miller's daughter became queen. She was given a throne right next to her husband, and learned to sit for long periods of time, as kings and queens do.

About two years afterward, a beautiful child was born and the little man appeared in the castle once again.

"Hi! I came for the kid," he said.

The queen jumped back and clutched her child to her chest.

"But you can't have my child! What will you do with him?"

"Dress him in a green suit and make a funny little old man out of him. What else?"

The queen imagined her baby in a little green suit and little pointed cap and began sobbing loudly. In fact, she sobbed so loudly the man decided to give her a second chance.

Pulling his fingers out of his little ears, he said, "I'll tell you what. I'll make a deal. If you can discover what my name is in two days, you can keep the child."

The little man paused. "Boy, won't this make a keen fairy tale someday?"

The queen began pacing the royal nursery and calling to mind all the names that she could think of.

"Are you Henry? Clyde? Newton? George, Marmaduke, Sidney, Frank?"

"Nah," said the man.

The queen then desperately searched for still other names. She looked in the village white pages, *Who's Who Among the Little People,* even the gossip column of the *Palace Chronicles.* The next day she tried again.

"Are you Ming Choi?" she asked. "Or Running Mouse? Cherry Nose? Charlie Brown?"

"No! You've failed," shouted the little man with a mischievous laugh.

"Well, what *is* your name then?" challenged the queen, her hands on her hips.

"It's, uh . . ." The little man took off his hat and scratched his head. "It's, uh . . ." Then a horrible realization came to him. He didn't know what his name was!

"Wait here. I'll be right back," he said to the queen. He dashed into the kingdom to see if he could find anybody who could tell him what his name was.

"Do you know me?" he asked the palace garbage collector.

"No. I can't say I do—and with any luck I never will," the garbage man replied, jumping into a garbage can and pulling the lid on top of him.

The little man asked everyone he chanced to meet, from the village moat cleaner to the royal jackhammer operator, but nobody could tell him who he was. Finally, out of desperation, he went to an old wise man who lived in a hole in the ground.

"No, I don't know your name," said the wise man in the hole in the ground. "But I know how you can find out. Get yourself a mailbox. Sooner or later, somebody will send you a letter. Then all you have to do is see what name is on the envelope."

That was it! He was truly a wise man—or at least as wise as anyone can be who chooses to live in a hole in the ground.

In any case, the little man did as he was instructed. He got a mailbox and waited inside for a delivery, and before long, he did receive a letter. It was from a talk show sidekick who told him he might have already won a million dollars. But that's another fairy tale. The little man just wanted to see what his name was. But when he saw it, he was shocked. It read "Rumpelstiltskin."

"Rumpelstiltskin!" he cried. "What kind of a name is that? I can't go back to the queen and tell her my name is Rumpelstiltskin. I'd be the laughingstock of the kingdom."

And so, the queen and her child lived happily ever after, for she never saw the funny little man in the green suit again. In fact, nobody ever saw the little man again, because he was so ashamed he got out of the magic business and changed his name to Louie Smith.

And we all know there's never been a fairy tale about Louie Smith.

That is, until just now.

THE ENCHANTED
GNAT

here was once a tinker who had three sons. Freddy was a good boy, and Teddy was a good boy. But Nathaniel, the youngest—he was definitely not a good boy.

"Um, Nat?" asked the tinker one day. "Why did you throw that cake on the floor?"

"Well, you said it was a marble cake and I wanted to see if there were any marbles in it."

"Um, Nat?" asked the tinker another day. "Why did you toss that cat through the window?"

"Well, I just wanted to give him a little pane in the neck."

The years went by as they have a habit of doing, and the sons grew older and wiser. All except Nat. He grew older.

"Um," said the tinker another day, "who burned down the house?"

"I lit a fire in the fireplace," said Nat.

"But we didn't have a fireplace," sighed his father. "Remember my words, Nat. Someday you'll hang for all this."

Now you might think that a tinker's lot is a poor one. Far from it. Every day, the tinker would leave his sons and go find something to tinker with, and then he'd tinker for eight hours, with an hour's break for lunch. After years of this, he had become independently destitute. But one Christmas, he could afford to buy his sons a jukebox.

"Gee, Dad, it's a jukebox!" shouted Nat.

"Don't open the jukebox," said the tinker. "It's not that kind of box."

Too late. Nathaniel not only opened the jukebox, he bashed it against the wall. And there, standing amidst the rubble, was a little old man with a beard.

"Is your name Juke?" asked the tinker.

"No," said the little old man. "I'm a sprite who has been locked inside that music box for one hundred centuries. Have you ever been forced to listen to eighty thousand choruses of 'Freebird'?"

The sprite explained that, being a sprite, he was qualified to grant each of the tinker's three sons one wish.

The first son wished to be richer than anyone in the world and—P☺☺F!—there at his feet lay all the precious stones in existence. The second son wished to be married to the sweetest, most beautiful girl in the world and—P☺☺F!—he got a lovely young bride.

But Nathaniel was a different story.

"Look," he told the sprite. "You may fool the Bobbsey Twins over there. But not me. There's nothing to wish for. I just want to be me . . . Nat!"

And—P☺☺F!—there was a puff of smoke

and Nat had gotten his wish. Sort of. He had become a gnat.

"This is terrible," said the tinker, watching his son buzz around the room. "I beseech you, return Nat to his former self!"

But the sprite was exhausted from all his wish granting. The best he could do, he told the tinker, was try again after a month's rest. But Nat wasn't about to wait around. Out the window Nat flew. Not very far from the tinker's house was an old hut that belonged to a witch, and Nat figured that the witch could change him back to his former self. But in the midst of his flight, he chanced to pass over an elderly woman who was having a picnic.

"Long as I'm a gnat, I might as well have some fun," thought Nat. And with that, he dive-bombed the lady. He zoomed in, she swiped, she lost her balance, and, splat, she planted her face right in a custard pie. Nat, who liked a good slapstick joke as well as the next guy, burst out into his whiny little laugh, then continued on his way, making a beeline, or rather a gnatline, to the witch's hut.

But when he got there, the witch was nowhere to be found. The reason was that the witch was out having a picnic. That's right, that elderly lady with pie on her face was actually the witch! And when she came back, she was mad as heck.

"If I ever lay my hands on the gnat that spoiled my pic . . ." She stopped in her tracks. "Ha! There you are, you little pest!" And with that, she trapped Nat under a glass.

"Oh spare me, Ms. Witch!" cried Nat in his tiny

voice. "I'm not really a gnat, but Nathaniel, son of the tinker, put under an evil spell!"

"Nathaniel?" said the witch, raising her eyebrows. "You're not the mean little kid who's the scourge of the neighborhood?!?!"

"Yes, that's me," admitted Nat.

"Boy, if I had a son I'd want him to be as nasty as you. Us witches are proud of your work!"

And with that, the witch said she'd be proud to change Nat back to his former self. When the newly human Nathaniel returned to his father, he picked up where he left off.

"Um, Nat?" asked his father. "Why did you hook the cow up to the reducing machine?"

"I wanted a milk shake," replied Nat.

Three weeks went by and then came the night the sprite had promised to return. "I don't have any wishes, Mr. Sprite," said Nathaniel. "Like I said before, I just want to be me!"

"Don't say it again, Nat," warned his father.

"Don't worry, Pop," said Nat, holding up a document. "You see this? I had my name changed to Arthur. So I just want to be me—Art!"

With that, the sprite pointed his finger and—POOF!—Nat became Art. A work of art, that is. An abstract expressionist painting in a gilded frame. Not a bad painting, actually—but that's off the subject. The tinker was crushed. But strangely enough, the tinker's prophetic words had come true. He said that someday Nat would hang. And so he did. On the living room wall.

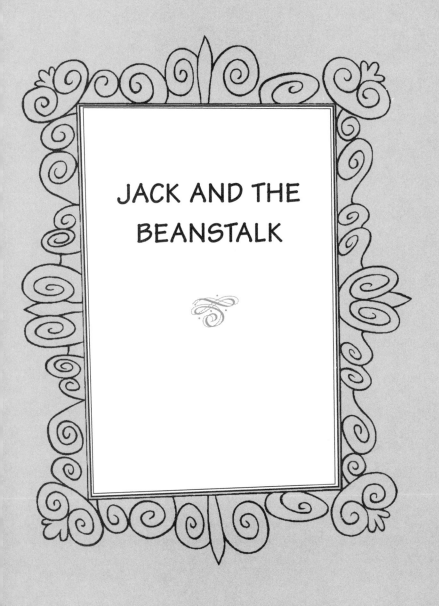

JACK AND THE
BEANSTALK

nce upon a time—actually, it was 1888, but this isn't a history textbook, you know, so we don't have to get all boring and technical. Once upon a time, there was a young lad named Jack. Jack had come to the big city to try out for a baseball team, the Boston Beavers. The Beavers were a great team, managed by that legendary figure, Big Lip Leo.

Listen as Leo gives one of those legendary pep talks. "Men, we got a great ball club here. There's only one little thing that keeps us from being the top team in the country . . . We've never won a game."

True, the Beavers had lost 597 consecutive games. But then again, they had never had Jack on the team. Now, Jack wasn't exactly your garden-variety baseball player. He didn't chew tobacco. He didn't scratch himself in embarrassing places. He didn't show up for "Yell at the Umpire" practice. And strangest of all, he had never played baseball before and knew not a single thing about the game.

"Hey coach," he would shout. "When do I get to make a touchdown?"

"No," the coach yelled. "Just run, *run!*"

"Ummmm. Where would you like me to run?"

It didn't look good. But hard as it is to believe, Jack wasn't as dumb as he sounded and looked. He had an ace up his sleeve, an ace he got to show at the season opener. The Beavers went up against the Poughkeepsie Pirates, who would probably play better if they stopped wearing those eyepatches and drinking rum. Anyway, it was the bottom of the ninth, the Beavers led 4 to 3 and needed just one more out before they won the game.

The Pirates' best player stepped up to the plate—or, actually, limped up to the plate, as he had a peg leg. The pitch, and *crack!* The ball sailed high over center field.

"What a hit!" shouted the announcer. "That ball is going, going. Hey, what's this?"

For at that moment, Jack pulled a magic bean out of his pocket, planted it in center field, watered it, and jumped on top of it. Rumble, roar, and whoosh! Jack was carried skyward on a huge beanstalk that grew straight up into the air. That fly ball landed smack in his mitt.

"Yerrrrr out!" shouted the umpire.

The fans went wild. The Boston Beavers had finally won a game. Of course, some of the Pirates weren't all that overjoyed and began showing the Beavers some extreme close-ups of their knuckles and cleats. But the rule books said nothing about banning beans. So the decision stood.

In the weeks that followed, the team won game

after game with the help of Jack and his magic beans. In fact, Leo changed the team's name to the Boston Beans. The guys in the stands started selling beans along with franks. And Jack became a national celebrity, getting his picture on the front of *People* magazine, *Sports Illustrated*, and *Legumes Weekly*. ("Bean There, Done That!" read the cover.)

Then came the big day for the final game of the season—the Beans were to play the Giants. It's no coincidence they were called the Giants. You could install observation decks on their foreheads and charge five bucks for entrance. It was going to be a rough game.

"Why couldn't we play the Plattsville Midgets?" whined Leo. "Or the Nantucket Napoleons? Or even the San Diego Men of Average Height?"

But the Giants it was. And right from the start, it was a fight to the finish. The Giants smashed ball after ball over center field, but Jack always managed to zoom up on his beanstalk and catch them on the fly.

Both teams gave it their all, and the scores shot higher and higher. Finally, at the bottom of the ninth, it was all tied up, 66 to 66. The Giants had the bases loaded, and Whitie Goober, their best hitter, came to the plate.

Whoosh! He let the first pitch go by. Whoosh! He let the second pitch go by. Two strikes on him. On this last pitch, Jack reasoned, Whitie would swing for the fences! Figuring he should prepare, Jack planted three beans, hopped on top, and shot up into the sky on the biggest beanstalk of all.

"Take that, Mighty Whitieeeeeeeeeee!" he yelled.

But Mighty Whitie, instead of slamming the ball, just gave it a dainty tap, and it dribbled out into center field. Jack was too high to do anything. Two players scored and the Giants won.

"I goooooooooofed!" yelled Jack.

But no one could hear him. That big beanstalk carried him straight up into the sky for hundreds of miles until it finally poked through a strange cloud where Jack saw a huge castle and heard these mysterious, booming words:

"Fee, Fi, Foe, Fum! I smell the blood of an Englishman!"

Now if Jack were an Englishman, he'd be playing cricket, not baseball. But he had no time to make that correction. He had to deal with more pressing problems—namely some extremely large molars about to give him a chewing out. But that's another story.

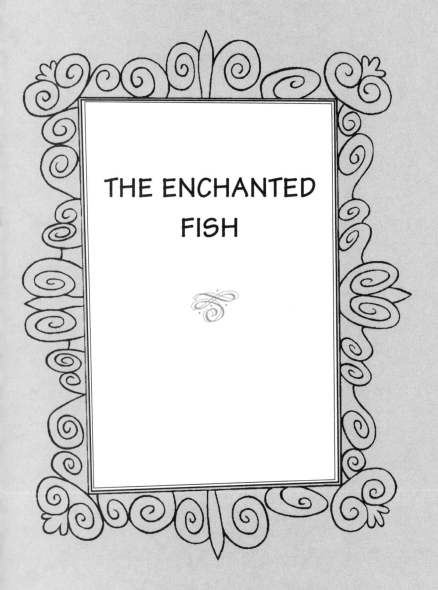

THE ENCHANTED
FISH

ong, long ago—about a year ago, actually—there was a little chimney sweep who was very, very poor. He was so poor he couldn't afford a name, so we'll just call him the little man. It was no mystery why he was poor: the kingdom had no chimneys, so chimney sweeping wasn't exactly a huge niche market. In any case, after an entire year, he only showed a profit of two cents. And that had been left to him by his wealthy uncle.

He decided to celebrate with a luxury he could only afford once a year. Food. Conveniently for our story, just down the block there was a fish store with a sign in the window "Day-Old Fish . . . Two Cents."

"I'd like a day-old fish, please," the little man told the storekeeper.

"That'll be two cents."

The little man proudly took the two pennies from his ragged pocket.

"Plus tax," said the storekeeper.

He frantically searched his pockets, but the little man just didn't have the necessary 16 cents. The storekeeper just shrugged his shoulders.

"Sorry, fella," he said. "But you know what? Since I like you, I'll give you this seven-day-old fish."

With that, he took out a week-old mackerel. An overpowering aroma filled the shop, and the little man became dizzy.

"What's that odor?" gasped the little man.

"I don't smell nothing," said the storekeeper. But it was hard to hear him. His gas mask muffled the words.

The little man edged closer so he could listen better.

"This here is a magic fish," said the storekeeper. "You take it, and you will have good luck!"

So the little man took the fish back to his spare but attractively furnished hovel. He was about to cook the fish when a messenger from the palace entered bearing a message.

"Is your name L. Man? And what is that awful smell?"

"Yes it is, and that's my dinner," replied the little man. "What's up."

"The king is having a ball tonight, and you are invited as the guest of honor."

"Me? Guest of honor? But the king doesn't even know me."

"Well"—the messenger shrugged his shoulders—"that's a fairy tale for you."

The little man was amazed, but he was also still hungry. He was about to drop the seven-day-old fish into the skillet when suddenly, the old fishmonger's words came back to him: "I don't smell nothing." All right, those words came back to him, but those are irrelevant to the story. The fishmonger's other words came back to him as well. "Keep this fish with you, and it will bring you good luck." Okay, that's better.

In any case, the little man realized he must have been invited to the palace because of the fish, and vowed to keep it with him always. Promptly at eight, the little man arrived at the king's palace and the ball blossomed into an instant failure.

The guests left in droves, the palace was declared off-limits, and the kingdom's newspapers began writing nasty editorials.

"I've got to act and act fast," said the king. "Okay, little man. I hereby make you a prime minister and am sending you to serve in my brother's kingdom."

The little man was stunned, but once again the words of the storekeeper came back to him: "I don't smell nothing." Not those ones. Anyway, early the next morning, one of the king's fastest ships sailed out of the harbor. Aboard were sixteen cats, forty seagulls, one little man, and one eight-day-old fish. When the little man arrived at the new kingdom, he found it under siege. A flotilla of enemy ships was bombarding everything in sight. As new prime minister, his duty was to save the kingdom. But without a sword, all he could do was to draw his fish, now two weeks old. He boarded the enemy ship.

"Stop this bombardment!" he commanded. "Have you no sense of decency?"

Well, the attacking force did not have a sense of decency. But they did have an acute sense of smell. They retreated. Most rapidly, in fact. And the kingdom was overjoyed. They thanked the little man—although they wisely did it from a safe distance.

"Here's your medal!" shouted the king, throwing it from the shore onto the boat, where it bounced off the little man's forehead.

"Now I shall come ashore and minister primes for you," said the little man.

"No, no!" shouted the king to the boat. "As prime minister, your first job is to return to my brother's kingdom and deliver a birthday present to him!"

"A birthday present? What is it?" asked the little man.

"You!"

And with that, the little man was sent again across the sea. However, halfway home, he encountered a raging storm during which a terrible thing happened. The enchanted fish was washed overboard. The little man's aroma was gone—but so was his good luck.

The ship was smashed to bits by a gigantic wave and the little man washed ashore, weeks later, tattered and weak from hunger. Who should be on the beach but the king, who was celebrating his birthday by having a jousting tournament and weenie bake.

The little man, without his fish, was accused of being a weenie bandit and thrown into a dungeon. He realized if he was ever to rise to greatness again, he'd need another fish. Which just goes to show you, for those who aspire to greatness, "Fishing . . . might make it so."

KING MIDAS

nce upon a time there was a king named Midas. Even by kingly standards, Midas was a greedy king. All he cared about was gold, gold, gold, and let's see, oh yes, gold.

So he sent his tax collectors into the kingdom to do his gold gathering for him. As the people grew poorer and poorer from being taxed, Midas grew richer and richer. Finally, the people were reduced to living on turnips and nothing but turnips. For breakfast, they had bowls of turnip flakes. For lunch, turnip sandwiches. And for dinner, roast leg of turnip with turnip gravy. By the time they got around to dessert—turnip torte—they were plain sick of tubers.

As a result, King Midas began to get the funny feeling that people didn't like him very much. The teeming masses holding up signs that read "Off with King Midas's head!" didn't help. Not that he cared about them. But what he did care about was that he couldn't raise taxes.

"I need to do something to make people like me," declared King Midas. "Then I can tax them even more!"

So the king called a meeting of his advisers, from the prestigious advising firm of Bobble, Bangle, Bead, and Benson.

"Gentlemen," said the king, "I must be made more popular."

"Well, sire," piped up Benson, "I'm just talking off the top of my thatch, here. But what about lowering the taxes? We could—"

That, apparently, wasn't a very good idea. Two palace guards grabbed Benson and carried him off to the dungeon.

The next day, the king called a meeting of his new advising firm, Bobble, Bangle, and Bead.

"Let's put this idea on the rack and see how it stretches," said Bead. "What we'll do is point out your warm, human qualities."

"What warm, human qualities?" asked the king.

"Well, you must have some. Dogs, for instance. Everyone likes dogs."

"I hate dogs," said the king.

"I can see it now," said Bead. " 'Midas Loves Mutts' on posters all over the kingdom!"

"How much will it cost?" asked the king.

"Next to nothing, sire."

"Solid thinking."

So the plan was set in motion. It was announced that the king would set free all dogs in the royal dog pound. And sure enough, as the people watched, the king let all the dogs loose. It was a touching moment. Until the dogs ran wild and stampeded the people's houses, smashing their few personal goods in such a way that the insurance companies refused to pay for damages. The people let fly at the king with the turnips.

So the next day, the king called a meeting of his advising firm, Bobble and Bangle.

"Let's put this in the crossbow and see how it shoots, Midas," said Bangle. "What you'll do is slay a dragon!"

"Hmm," said the king, "won't that be expensive?"

"Not at all."

"You're deep, Bangle. Really deep."

So, on the appointed day, the king strode north to do battle with a fire-breathing dragon. Which, of course, wasn't a real dragon at all. It was a big balloon, much like the one used during the royal Thanksgiving Day parade.

"On guard, foul fiend," shouted King Midas, raising his ax. "Thus I . . . uh . . . Thus I . . . uh."

"What's the matter?" asked Bangle.

"I forgot my speech," said the king, hanging his head.

"Never mind the speech. Just swing the ax."

Unfortunately, even before he could swing the ax, the dragon sprang an air leak and deflated to about the size of a beach ball.

"He's a fake!" shouted the crowd, and let fly with the turnips. Now they didn't just despise the king. They actually hated him. The king called a meeting of his adviser, Bobble.

"Well, sire," said Bobble. "Let's just throw this in

the moat and see if it floats. What if we give you the so-called golden touch."

"Isn't that expensive?"

"Not if you just use this spray gun and this cheap gold paint."

"Good thinking, Bobble. Very penetrating."

The word spread in a flash. "Midas: 24 Karat Monarch!" the papers read. The king promised a big free demonstration, and people came from all over. And indeed, with one squirt, he changed everything into gold: hats, canes, bushes, pencils, rocks.

"If the king says it's gold, then it's gold," reasoned the people. "Hooray for King Midas."

Well, the king sprayed more and more things until everything in the kingdom looked as if it were made of gold. Midas, of course, was very popular. There was just one problem: since everybody had more make-believe gold than he could use, gold began to lose its value. Soon it took a wheelbarrow full of gold just to buy one turnip.

"Bobble, you've done it!" said Midas. "The people like me and I'm still the richest man in the kingdom."

"Uh . . . not quite, sire. The country has gone off the gold standard."

"What? Well, what is the standard now?"

"Uh . . . turnips."

Yes, turnips it was. And of course, everybody had some turnips. Everybody except the king, that is. With nothing but gold, he was the poorest man in the kingdom. The next day, he called a meeting of his advisers. But there was nobody there but him.

So King Midas had to move to a very modest

castle with a twin-sized bed and a moat about as deep as an October puddle. But he still has lots of friends and, of course, he still has the Golden Touch.

the end